AF597006

What The Tree Saw

Contents

DEDICATED TO

To the Big Girls

my circle of fully grown women

who do not make excuses.

Like the great Tree,

we have each other's backs.

We protect one another,

look out for one another,

and stand strong through every season.

This book is for us.

AUTHORS NOTE

When the pandemic pressed time into stillness,

the earth stepped forward with comfort.

Petals opened.

Colors returned.

And the ancient tree continued its watch, steady and unbroken, offering shade to us just as it did to the flowers.

My girlfriends and I found refuge in those walks.

What seemed like simple visits to a small garden became moments of spiritual grounding — a whisper from nature reminding us that life was still speaking.

This book is the story from the Tree's point of view, a guardian who has witnessed generations rise and fall.

May it help you see the quiet relationship woven between all living things, and the way the Creator's creations reflect and care for one another.

WELCOME INTO MY VIEW , TO MY NEIGHBORHOOD, INTO MY REALITY

I have stood longer than memory.
Through storms and summers, through laughter and silence.
When the world slowed and your doors closed, I remained—
roots deep, branches stretched, eyes wide to the sky.

Maybe you saw what I saw?
The struggle for light, for space, to be noticed.
Their lives are short compared to mine,
so I make it a point to see them—
their colors, their reaching, their fall.

I see their birth and their death,
even when you pluck them before their time.
And still, they bloom.
Every flower that opened beneath me carried a secret,
and I listened.

These pages are not my story alone,
but what I witnessed—
the stillness, the crowding, the light breaking through.
I am only a tree,
but I saw what you should have felt.

The immense beauty beneath my branches.

Turn the page and see what I saw.

PART I — THE FIRST MEMORY

I have stood in this soil long enough
to remember what the earth felt like
before your footsteps shaped it.
Long enough to know that roots,
not years, measure a life.

The flowers call me their God.
I do not correct them.
Not because I am holy,
but because their belief is gentle
and harms no one.

They inherited that name for me
from ancestors who opened their petals
a hundred seasons ago—
ancestors whose colors I still remember
even though time has softened the edges.

I was here before their lineage began,
before the first seeds were carried by wind
to rest at my feet.
I watched their great-great-grandmothers
rise shyly from the soil,
leaning toward my trunk
as if I were the morning sun itself.

The first thing a flower ever asked me was:
"Will you keep us safe?"

And though I cannot control sun or storm,
wind or hunger,
I stretched my branches wide
to give her the only promise I truly own—
I will try.

I have tried every season since.
When sunlight becomes a blaze,
I widen my shade so the young ones
do not burn their first summer.

When storms swell and lightning forks the sky,
I plant my roots deeper,
making myself a shield
so the rain reaches them as a gentle patter,
not the sky's full weight.

My leaves fall without my command,
but I whisper to them,
"Drop softly."
They do not always listen.
A leaf has crushed more than one fragile petal
before its time.
And each time,
I feel a ring deepen inside me,
etched with something like guilt.

Still—
the flowers forgive me easily.
Perhaps that is why their lives
seem brighter than ours.

I have watched whole lineages bloom and vanish.
Some in a single season.
Some in sprawling families
that stretch across decades.

I remember the roses—
the first ones.
Their roots once curled proudly
through the soil beneath me.
When the original bush weakened,
humans came with tools
and grafted her onto another stem.
She survived a little while longer,
but it was her offspring
who carried her beauty forward.

The young roses today
have no memory of her.
They believe they sprung from the earth
fully themselves,
gloriously original.

But I remember.
I remember how humans worked carefully,
grafting tenderness into survival.
I remember how the mother plant
faded quietly
while her daughters bloomed bright above her.

This is the way it has always been:
the living carried forward
by stories they never heard.
And I—
the old witness—
am the keeper of the parts
no one else remembers.

Now turn these pages
and walk through the garden with me.
See what I have seen.
Learn what I have learned
from generations of petals
who trusted me
more than any god
they could imagine.

Now walk with me through the garden."

"A blossom opens
not because the world is safe,
but because it hopes."

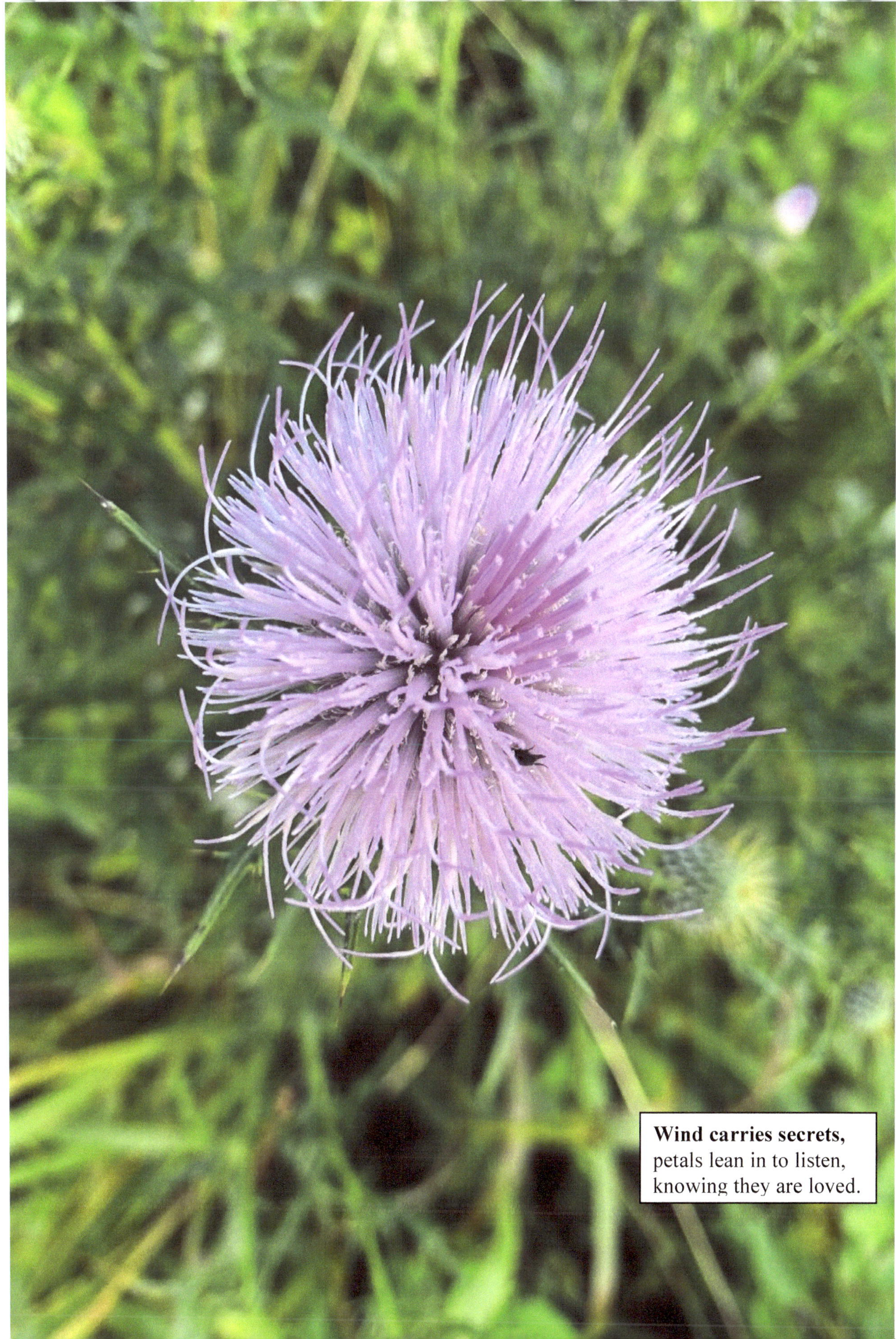
Wind carries secrets,
petals lean in to listen,
knowing they are loved.

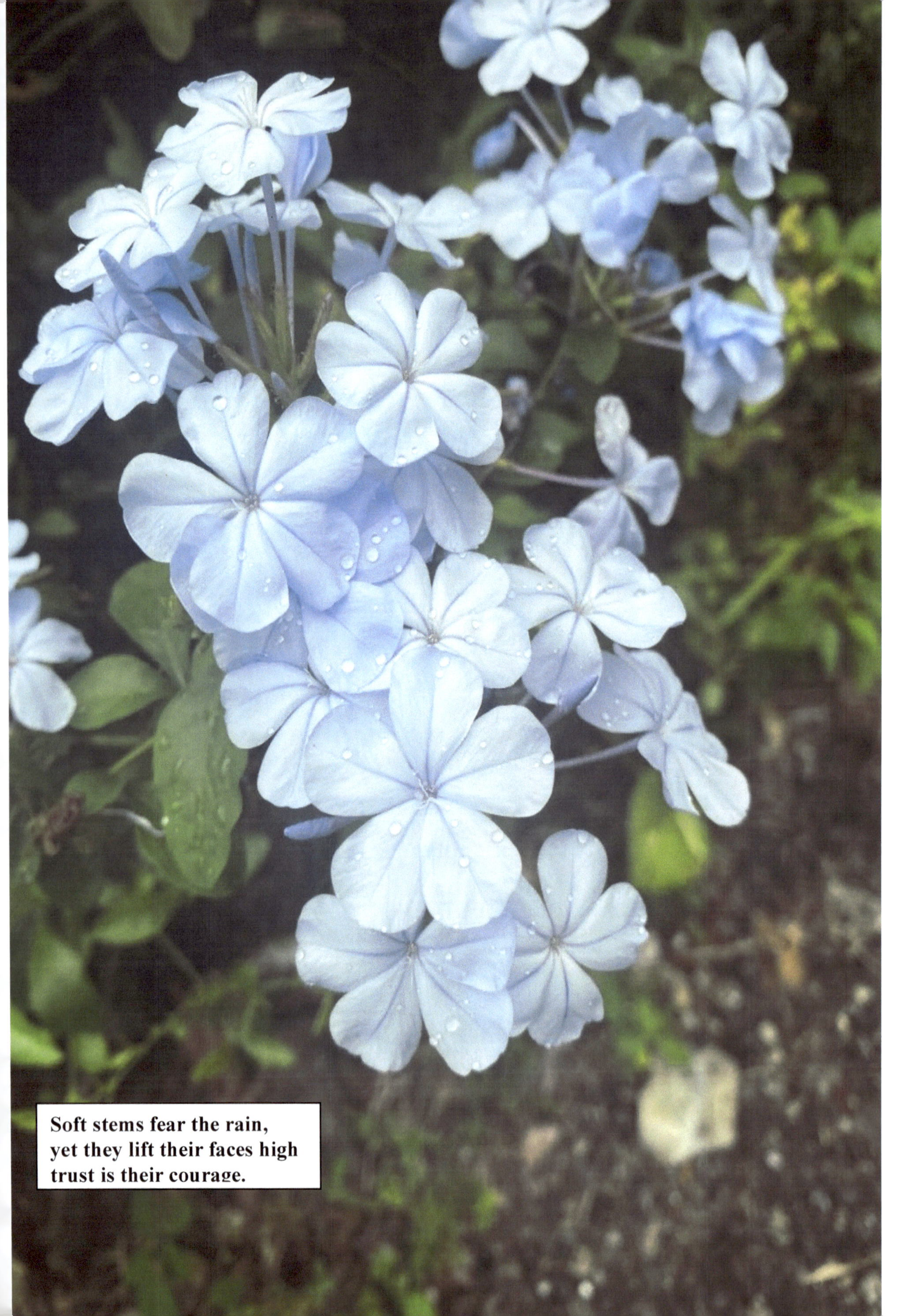
Soft stems fear the rain,
yet they lift their faces high
trust is their courage.

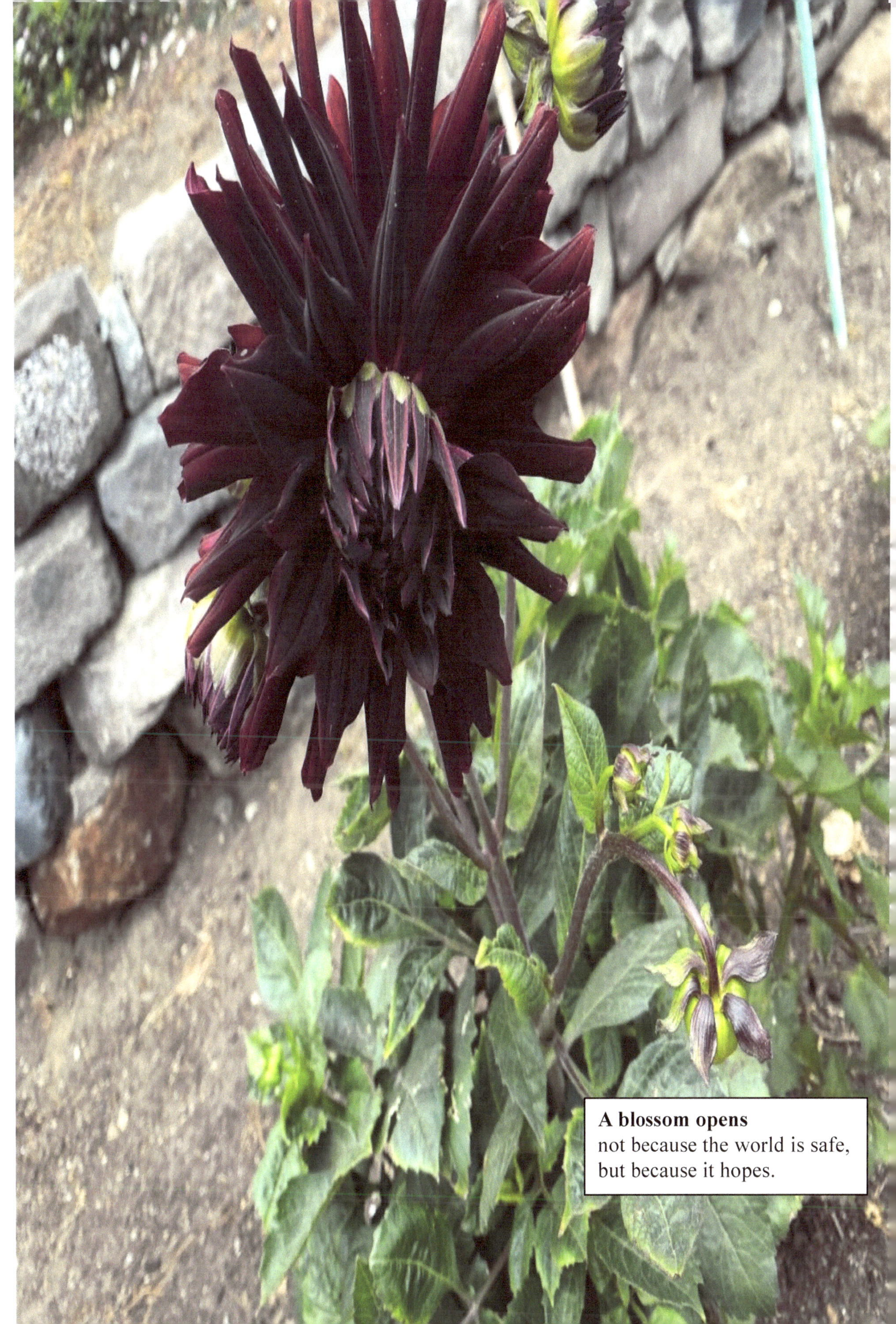
A blossom opens
not because the world is safe,
but because it hopes.

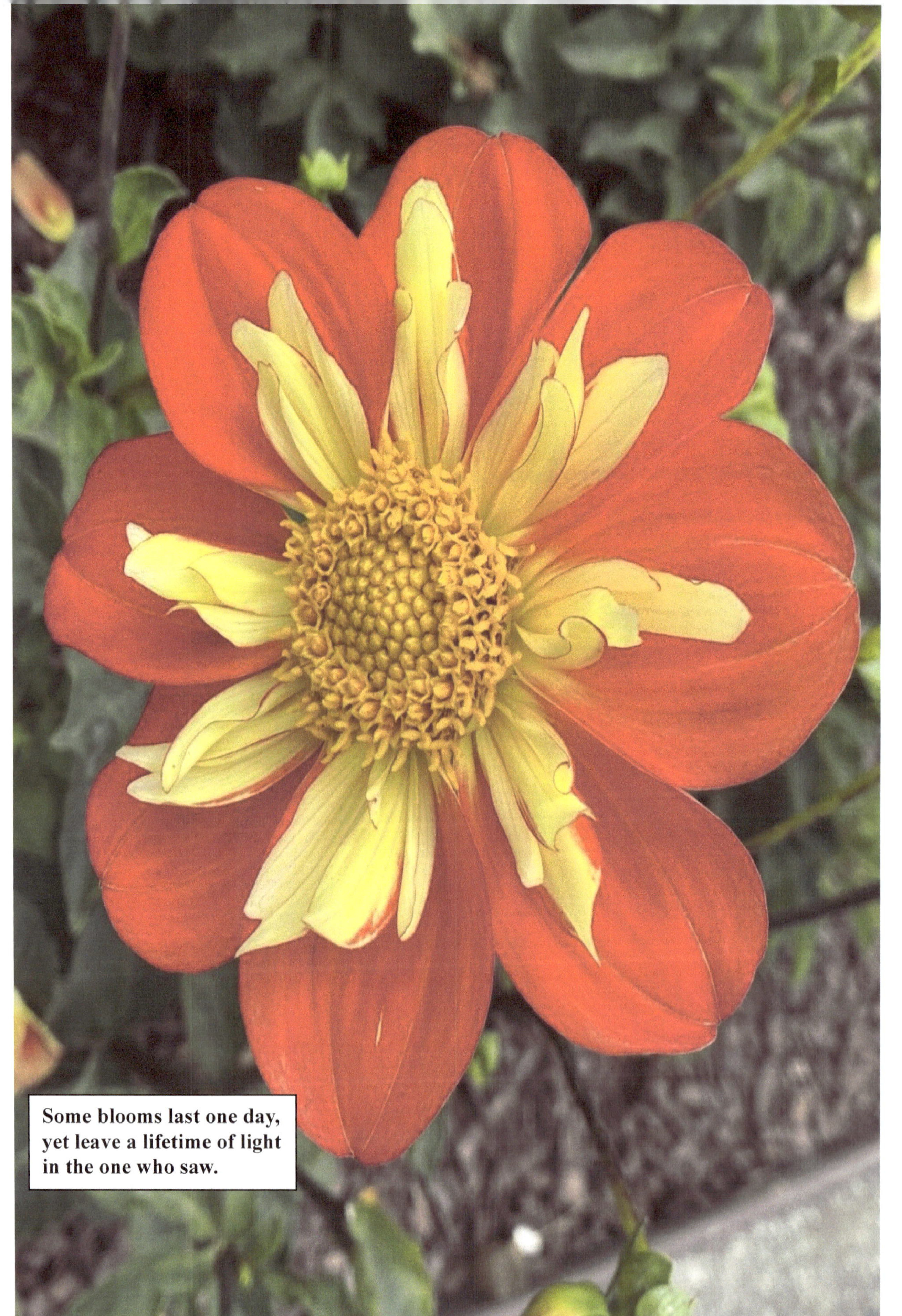
Some blooms last one day,
yet leave a lifetime of light
in the one who saw.

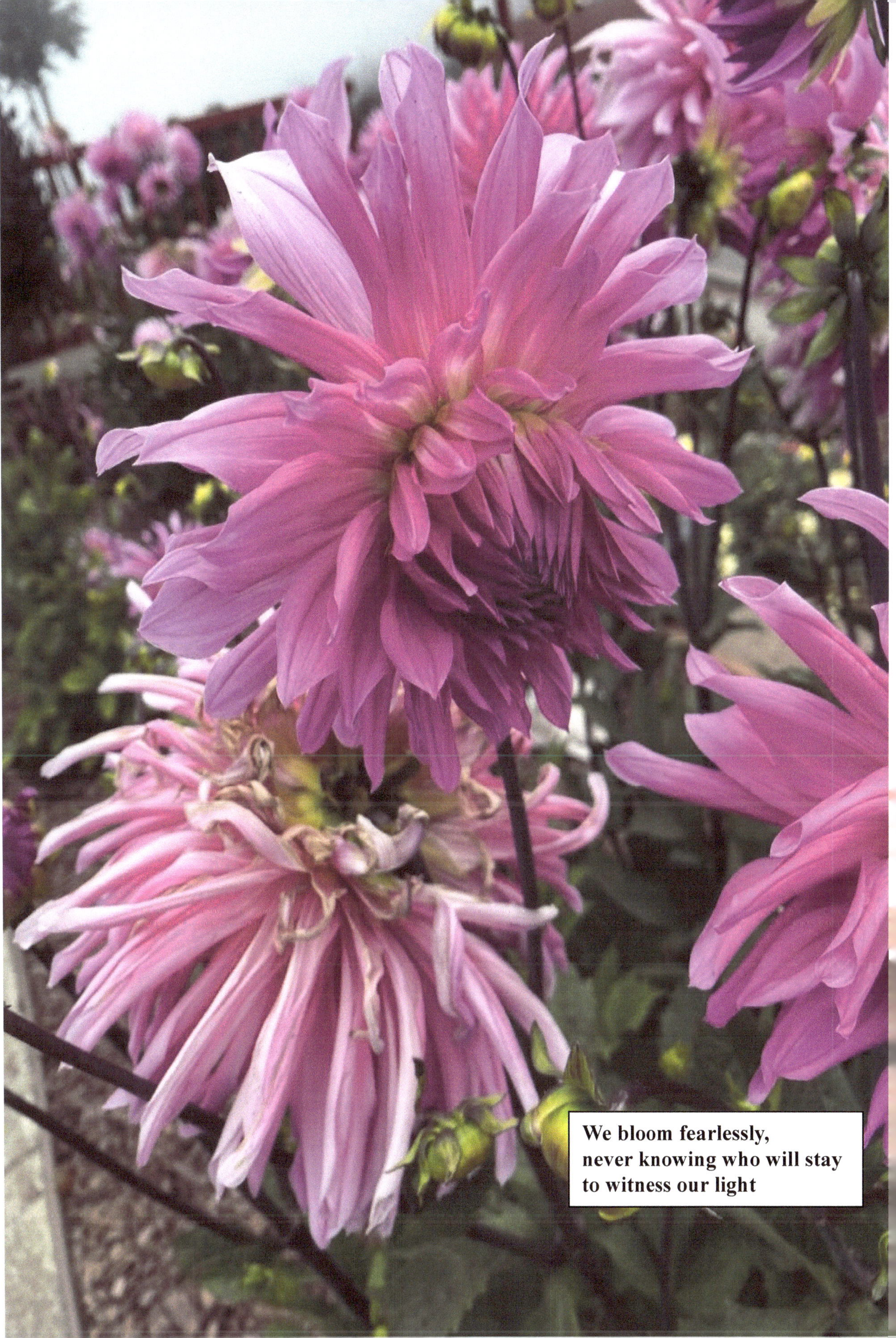
We bloom fearlessly,
never knowing who will stay
to witness our light

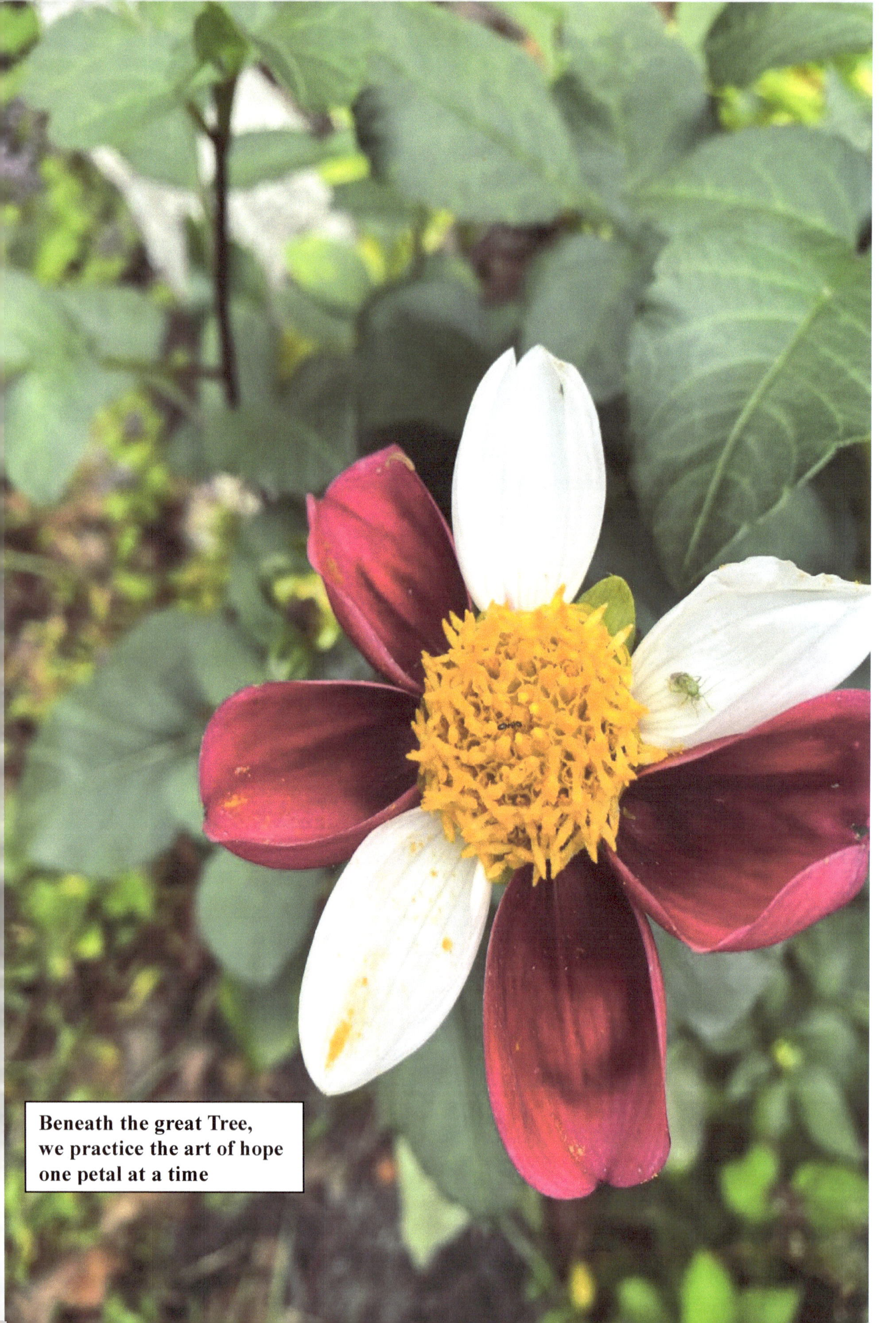
Beneath the great Tree,
we practice the art of hope
one petal at a time

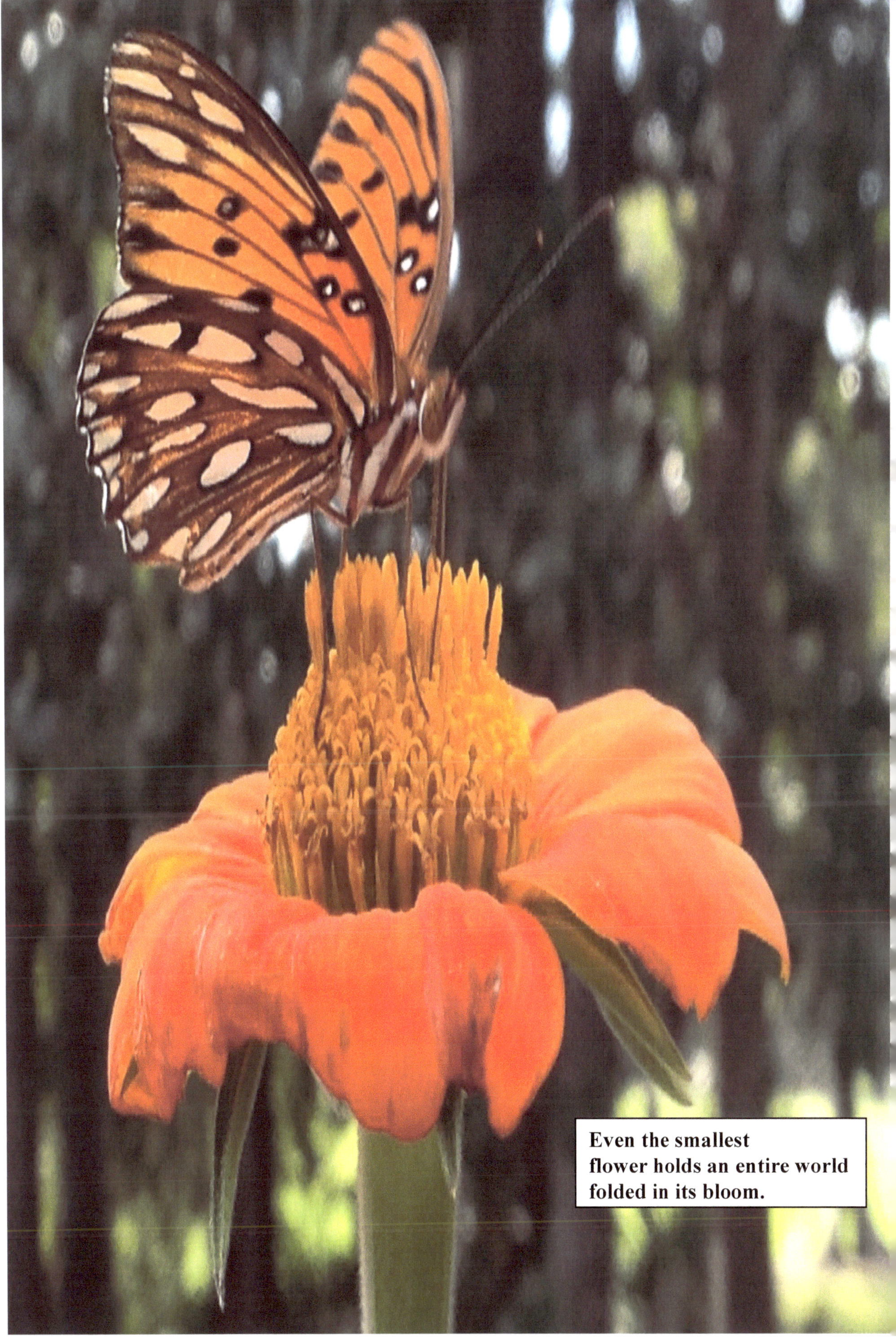
Even the smallest
flower holds an entire world
folded in its bloom.

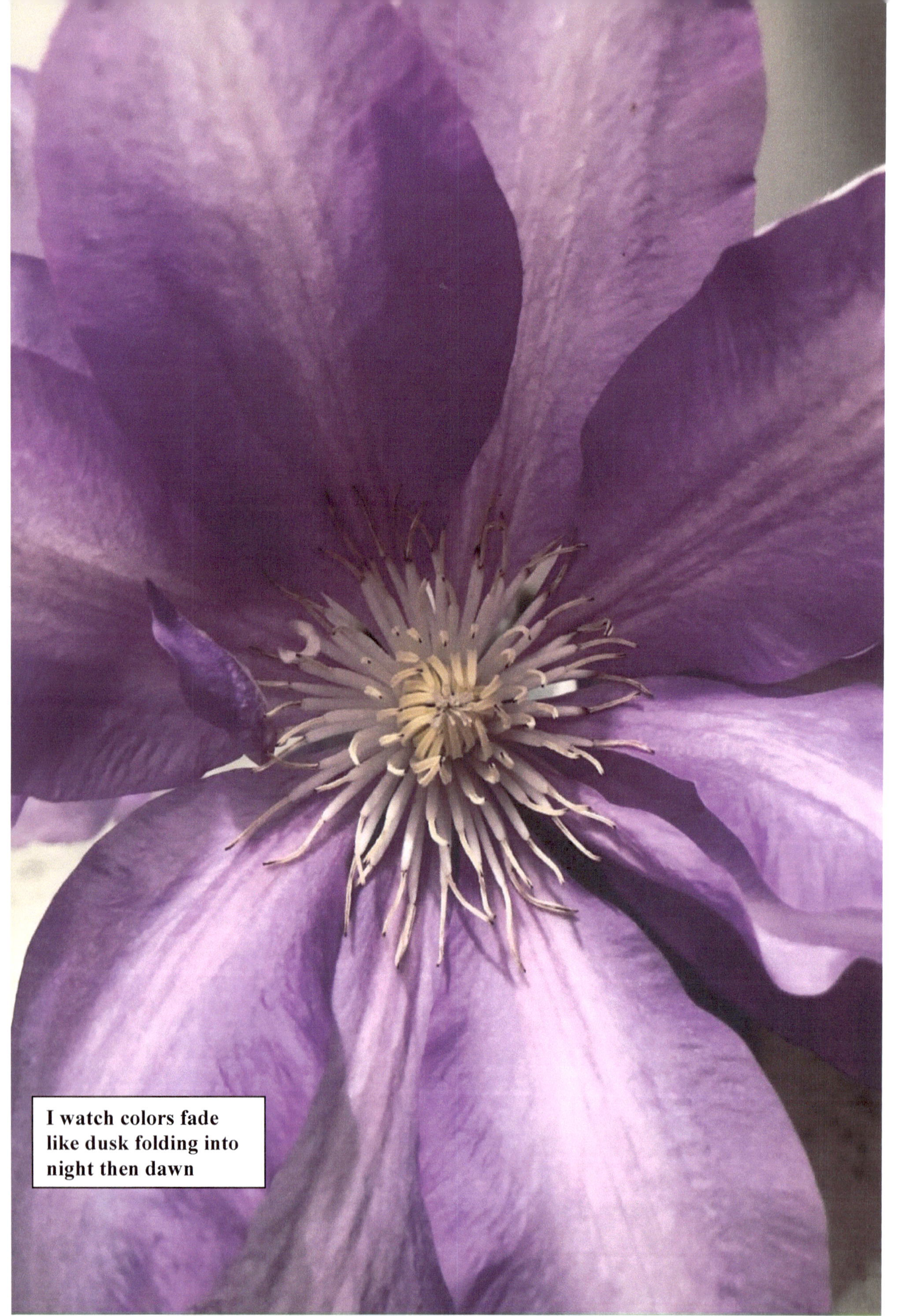
I watch colors fade
like dusk folding into
night then dawn

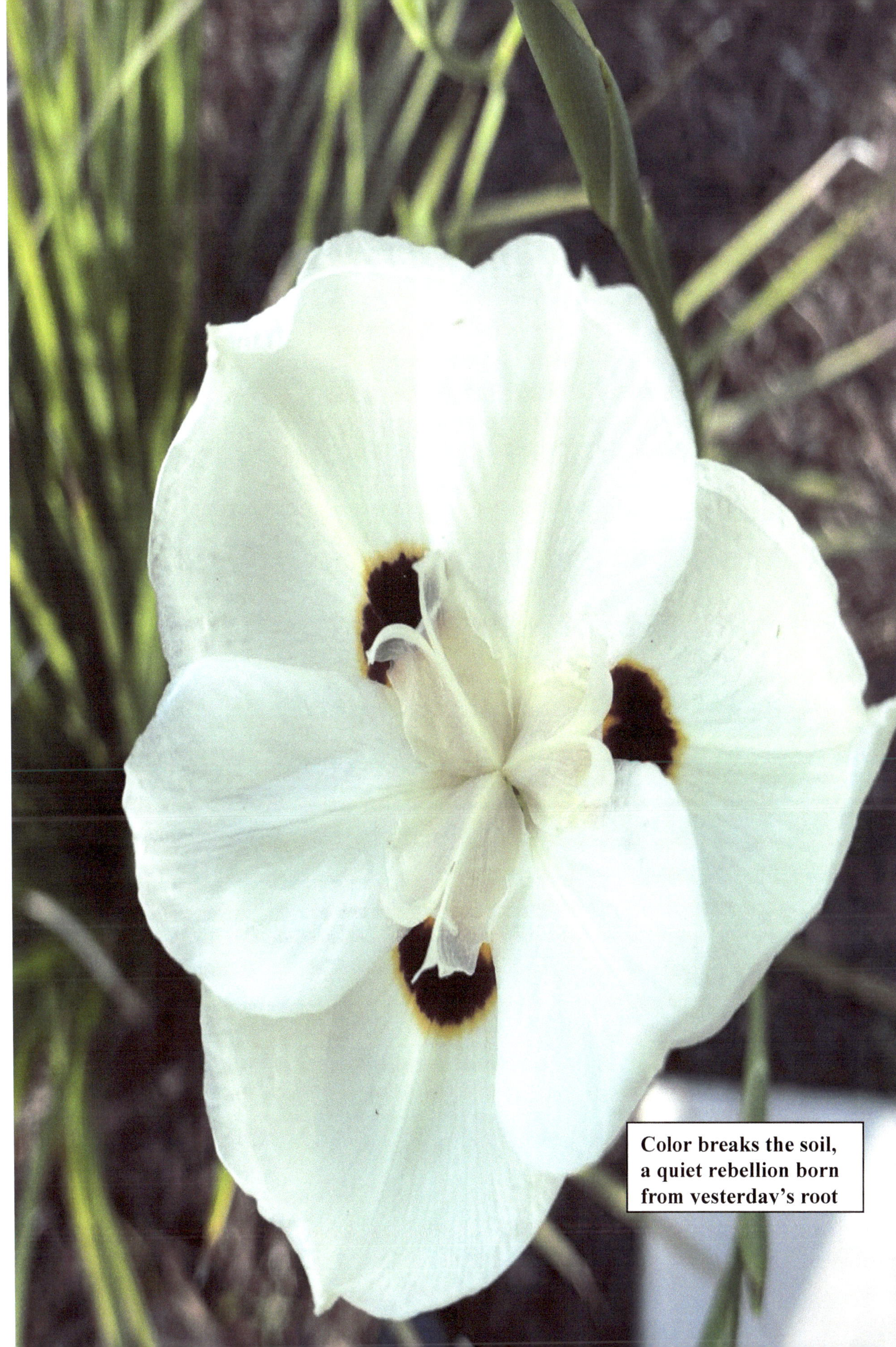
Color breaks the soil,
a quiet rebellion born
from yesterday's root

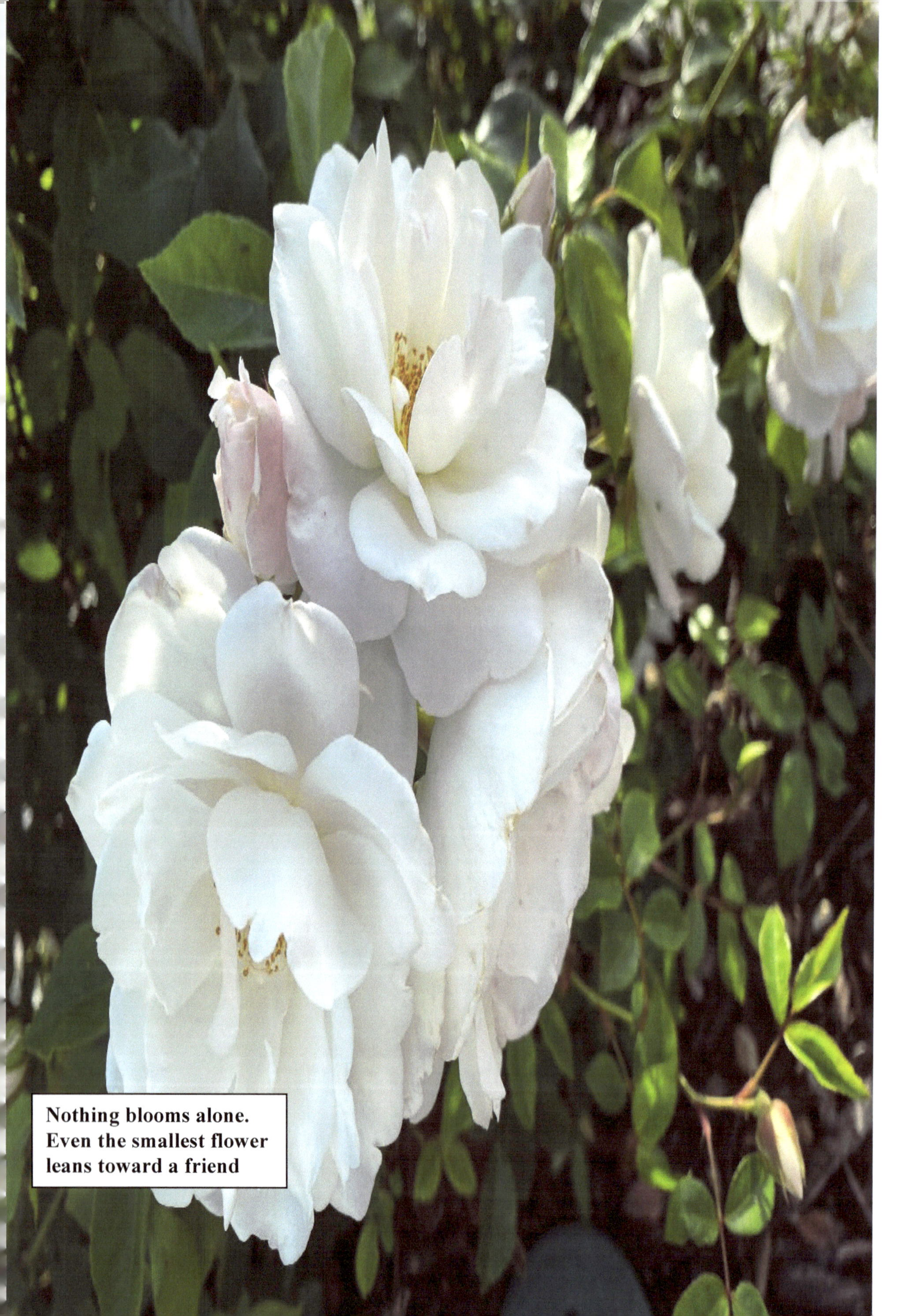
Nothing blooms alone.
Even the smallest flower
leans toward a friend

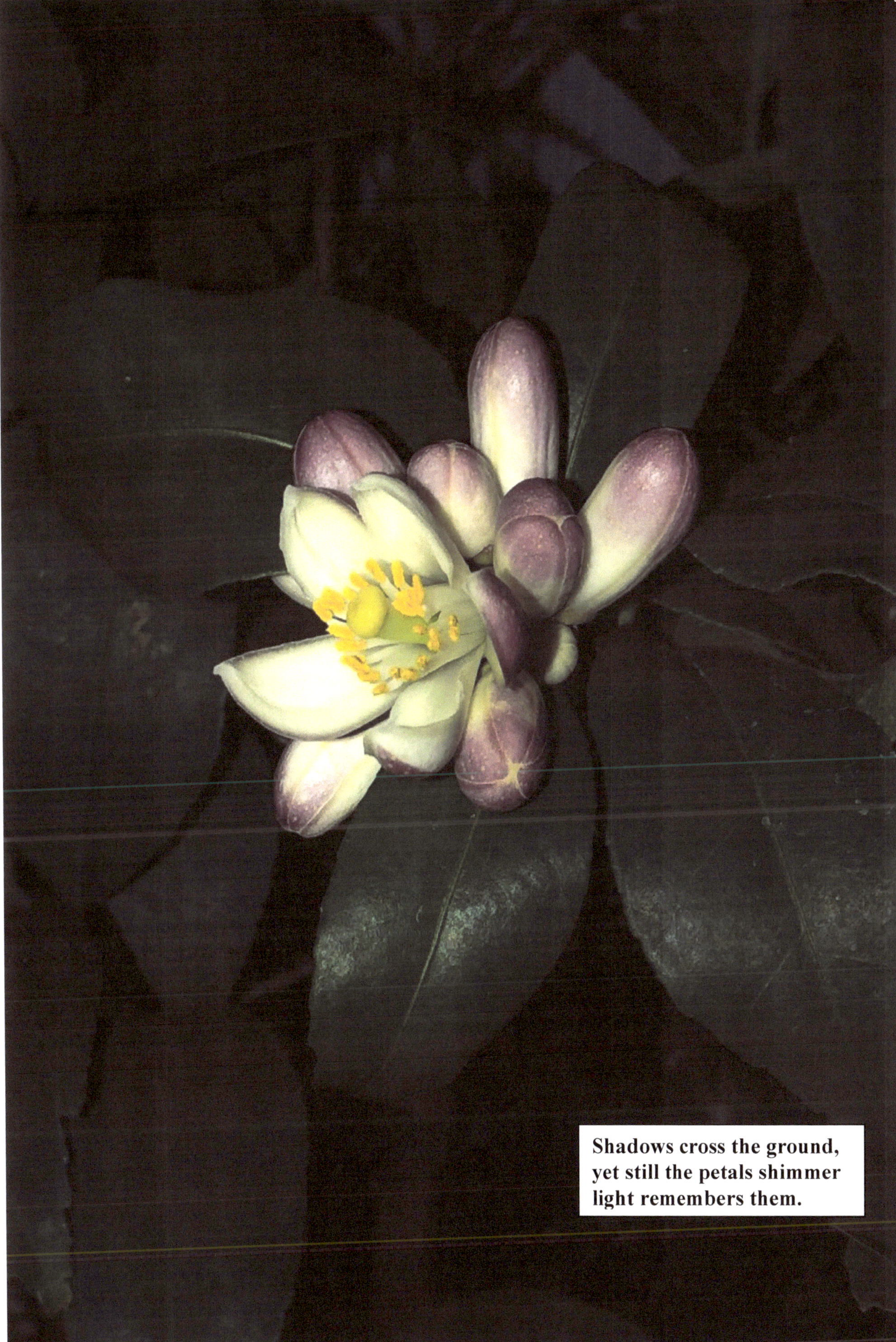
Shadows cross the ground,
yet still the petals shimmer
light remembers them.

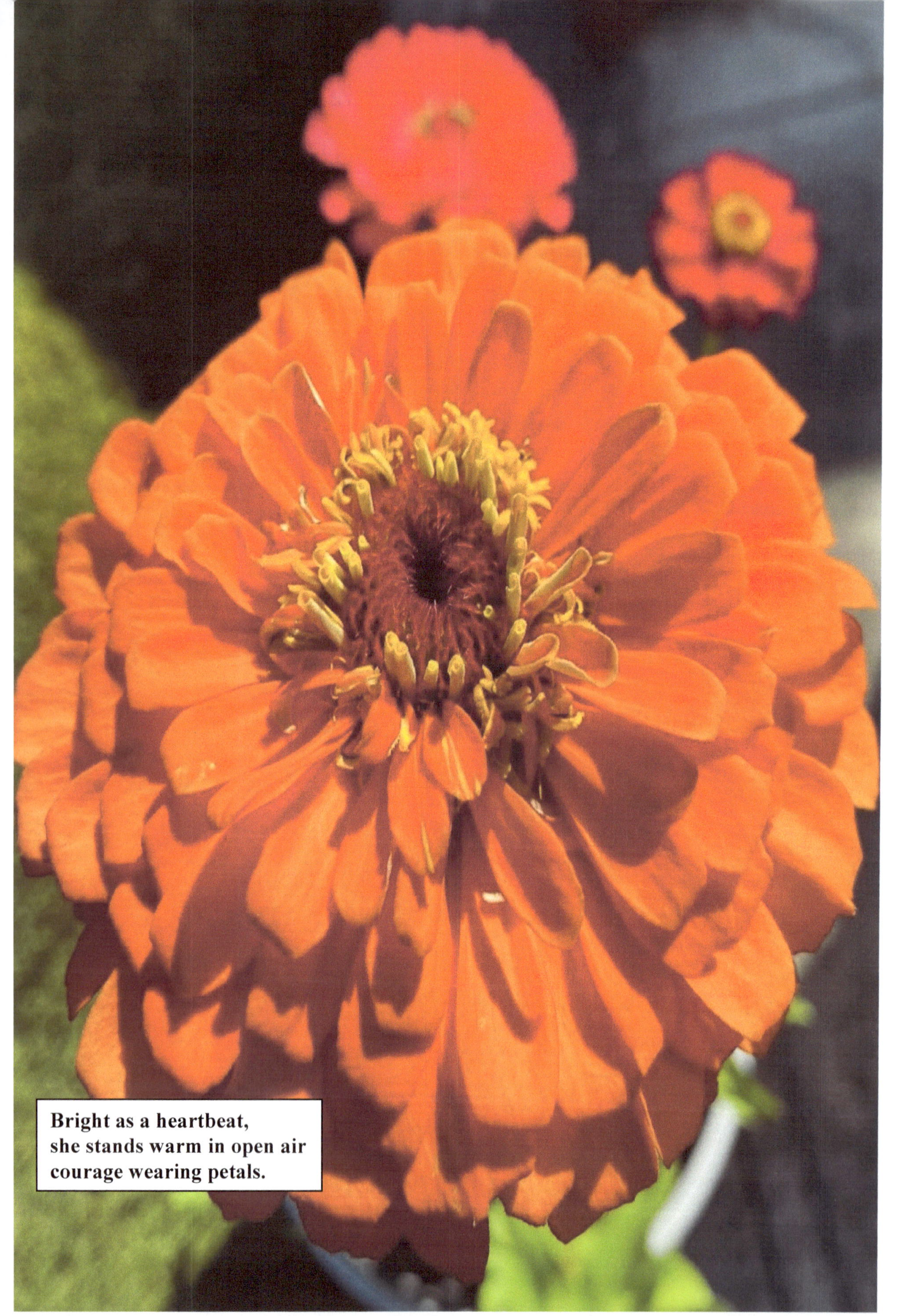
Bright as a heartbeat,
she stands warm in open air
courage wearing petals.

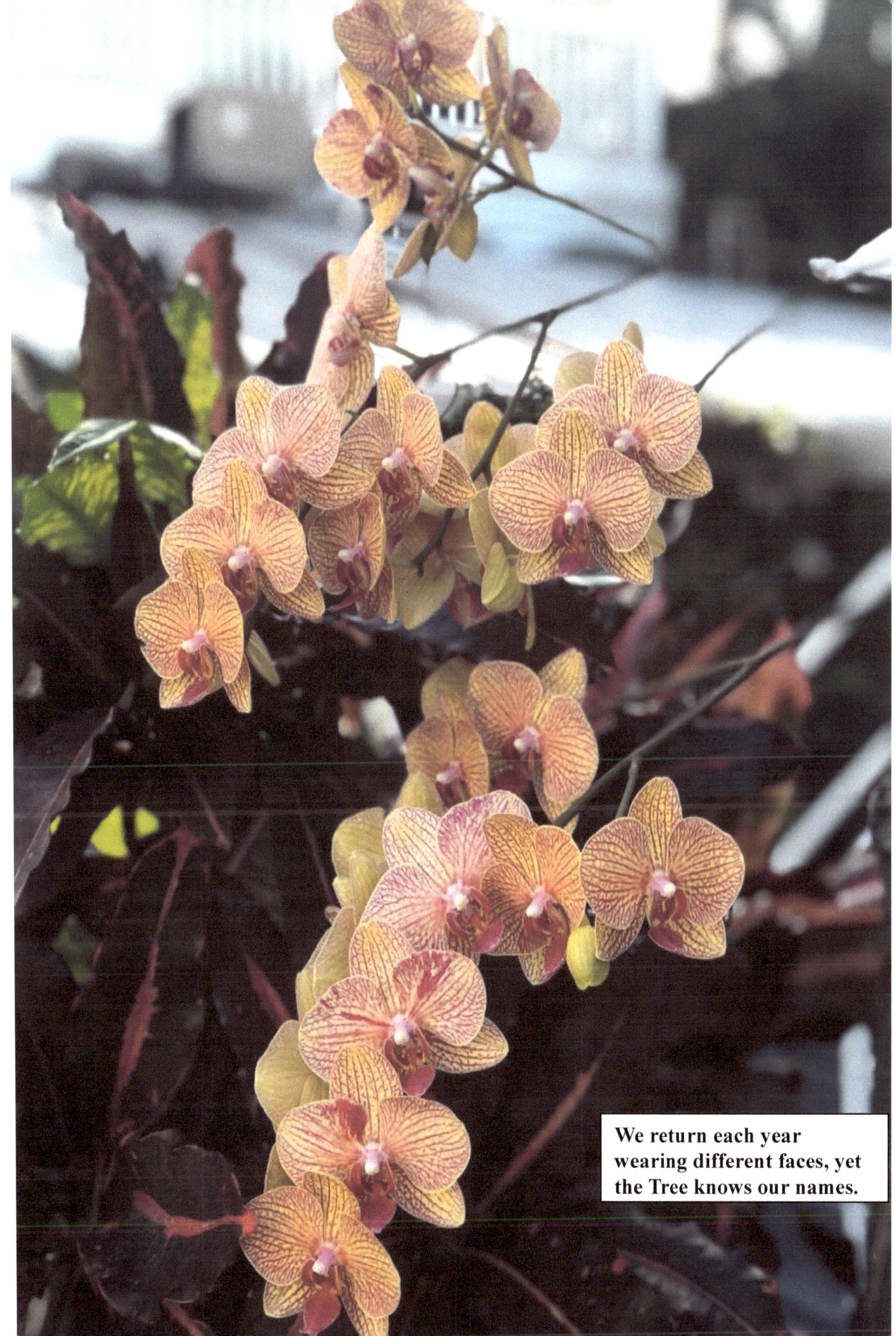
We return each year
wearing different faces, yet
the Tree knows our names.

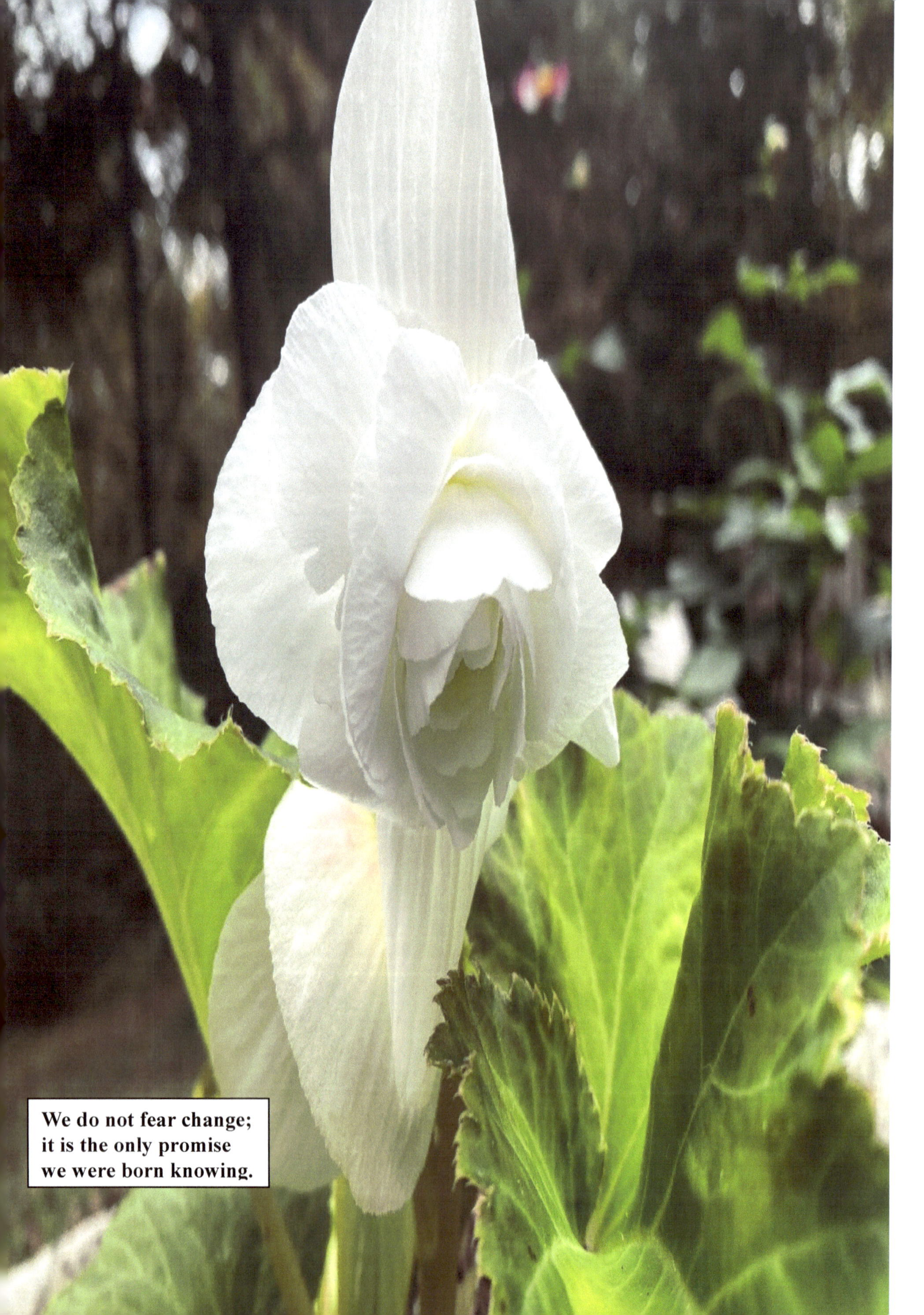
We do not fear change;
it is the only promise
we were born knowing.

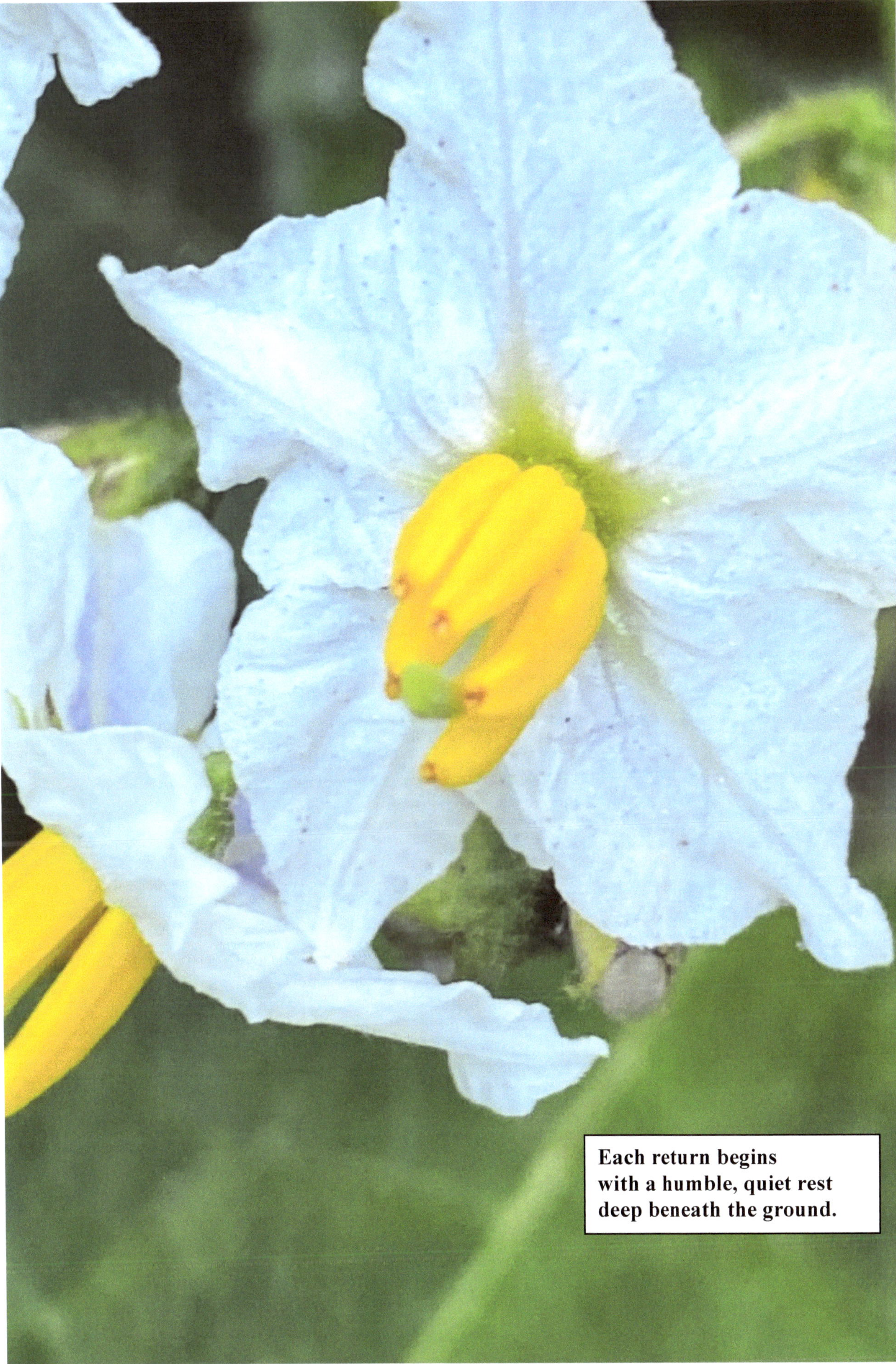

**Each return begins
with a humble, quiet rest
deep beneath the ground.**

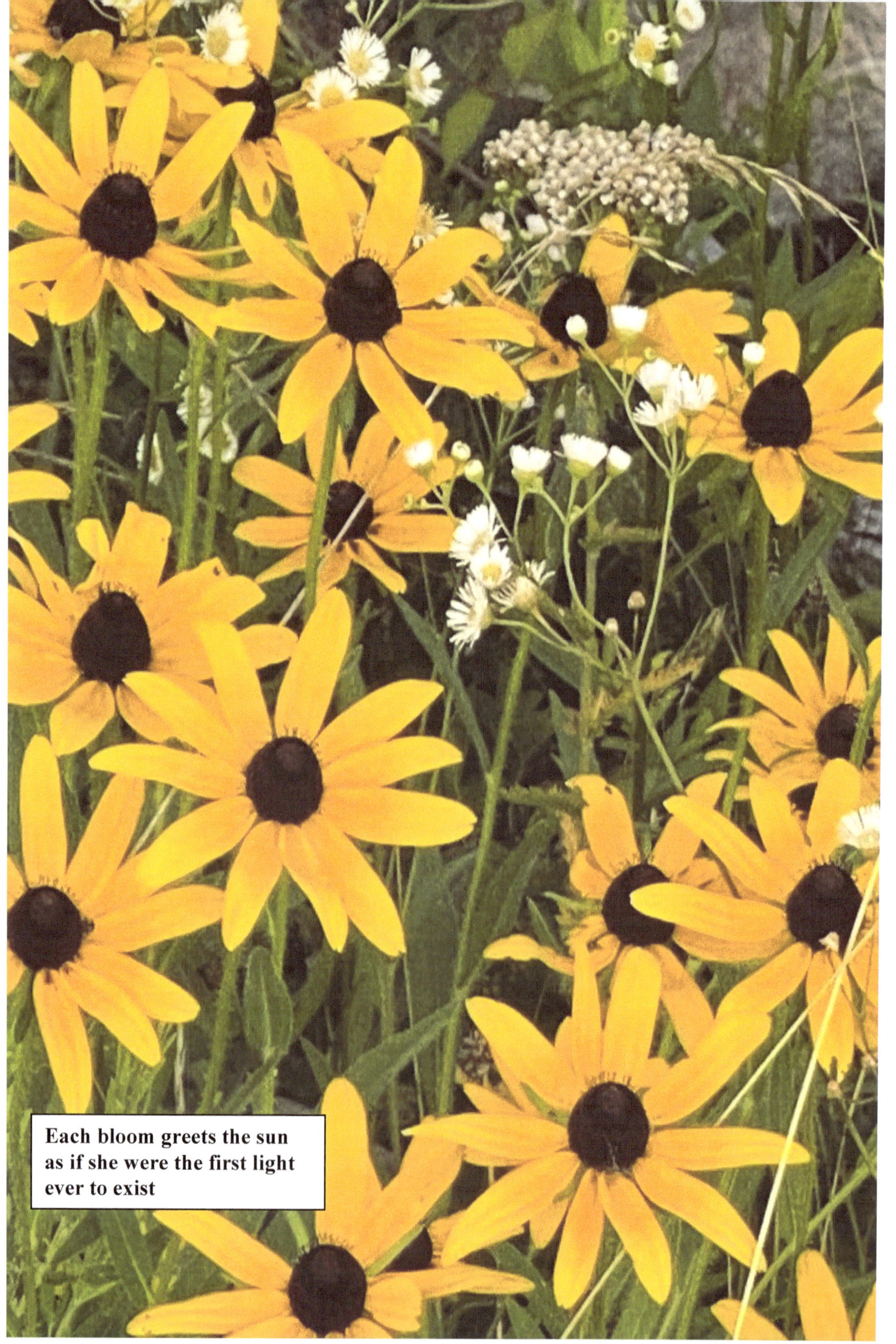
Each bloom greets the sun
as if she were the first light
ever to exist

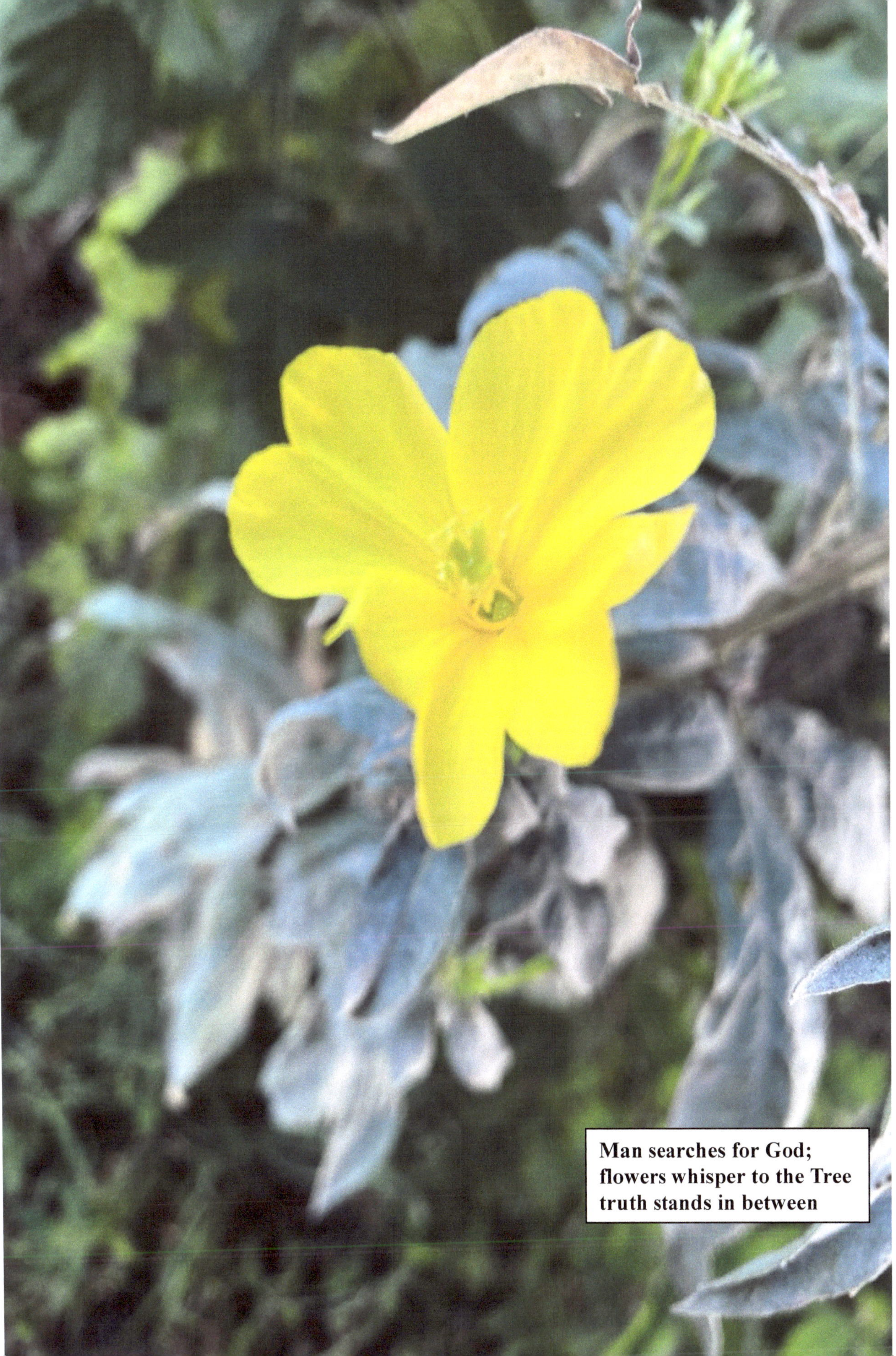
Man searches for God;
flowers whisper to the Tree
truth stands in between

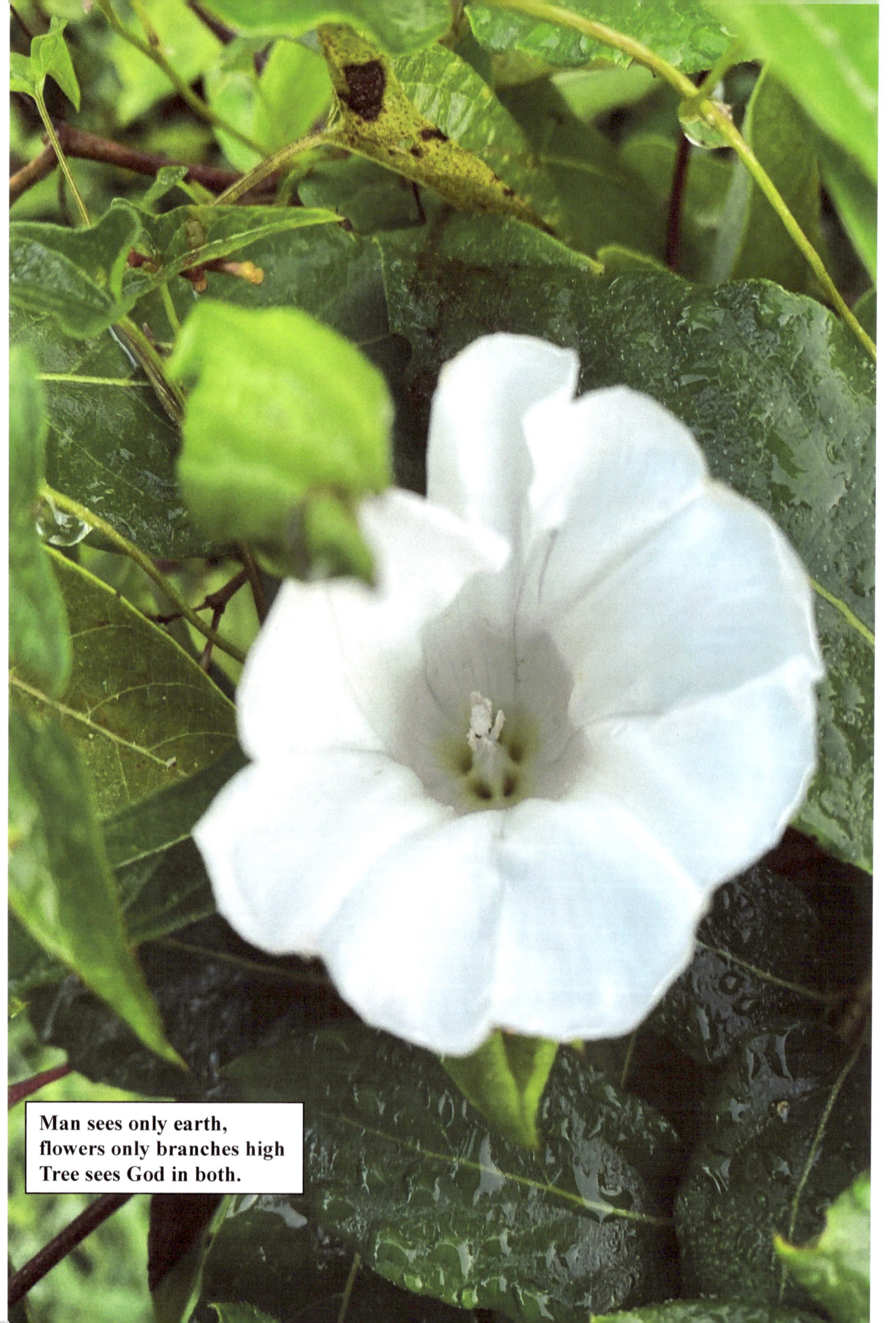

Man sees only earth,
flowers only branches high
Tree sees God in both.

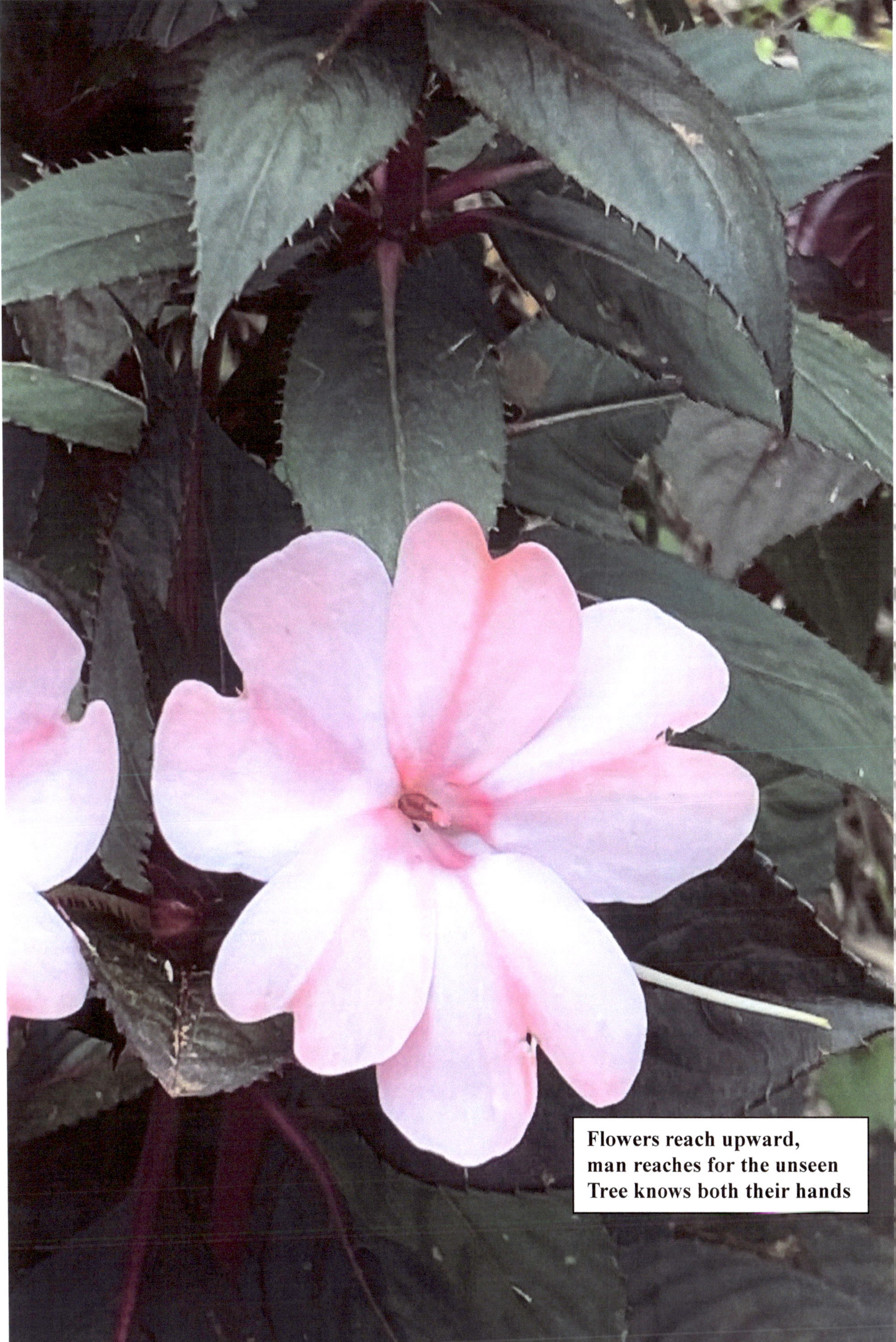
Flowers reach upward,
man reaches for the unseen
Tree knows both their hands

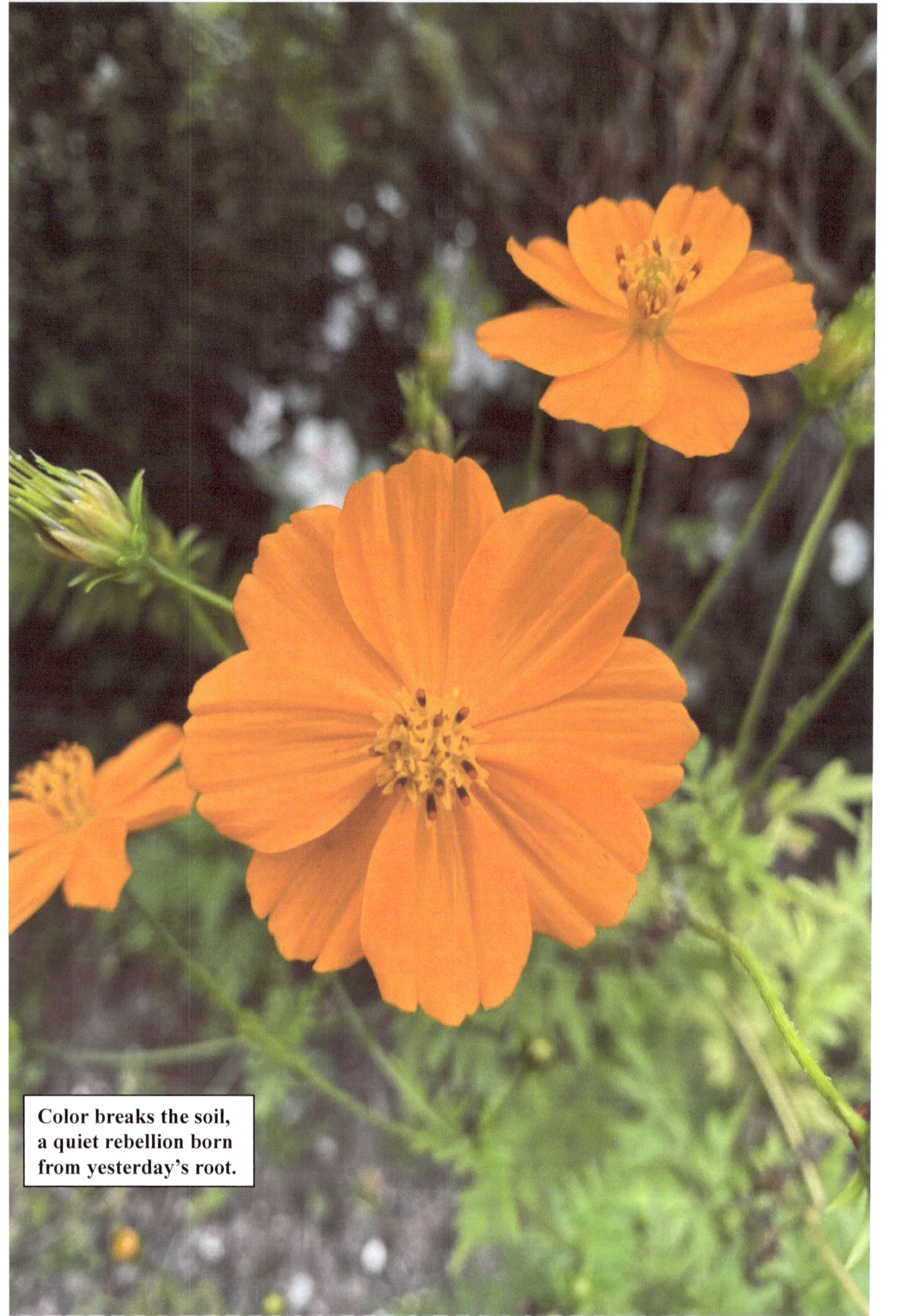
Color breaks the soil,
a quiet rebellion born
from yesterday's root.

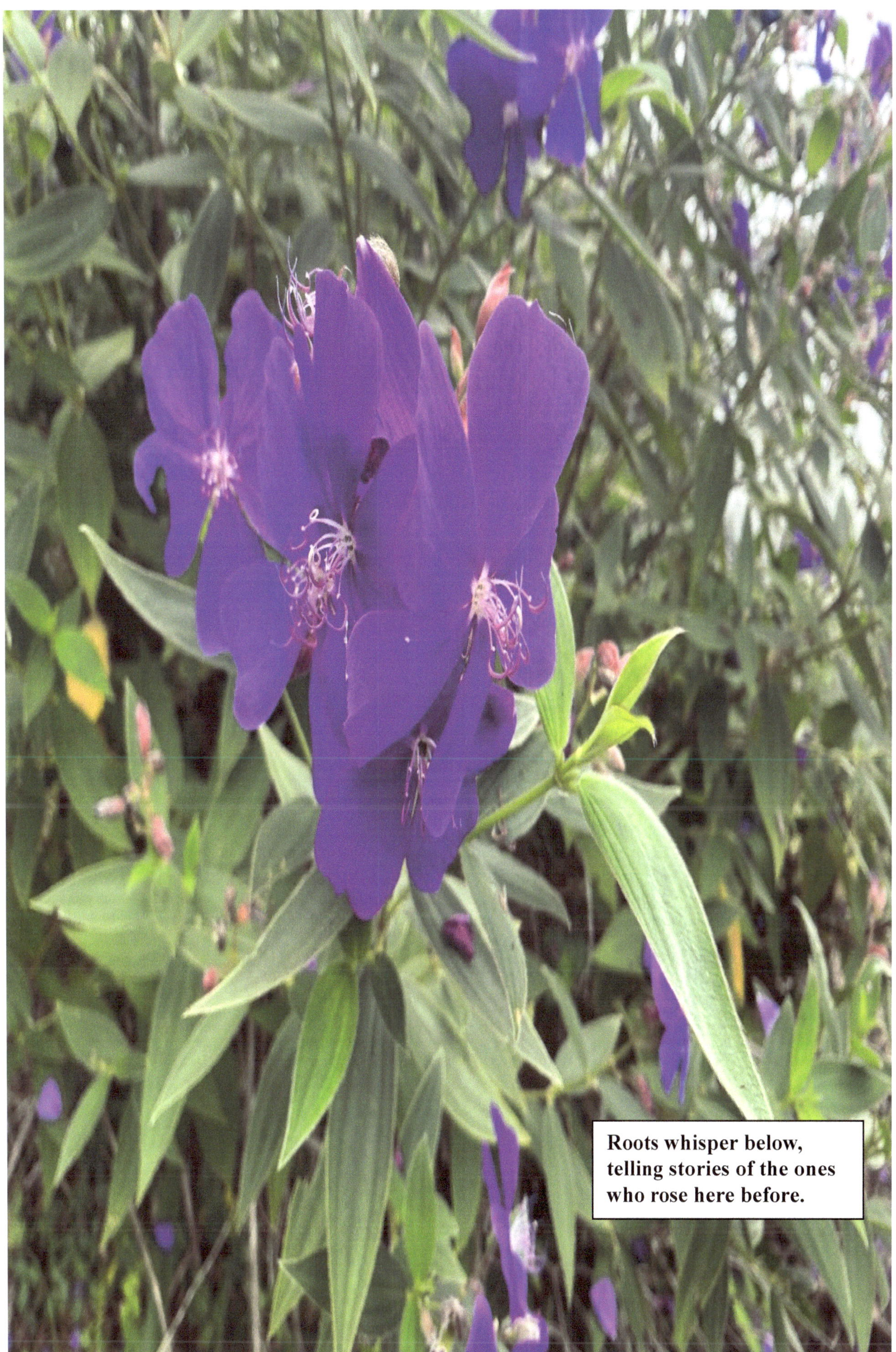
Roots whisper below,
telling stories of the ones
who rose here before.

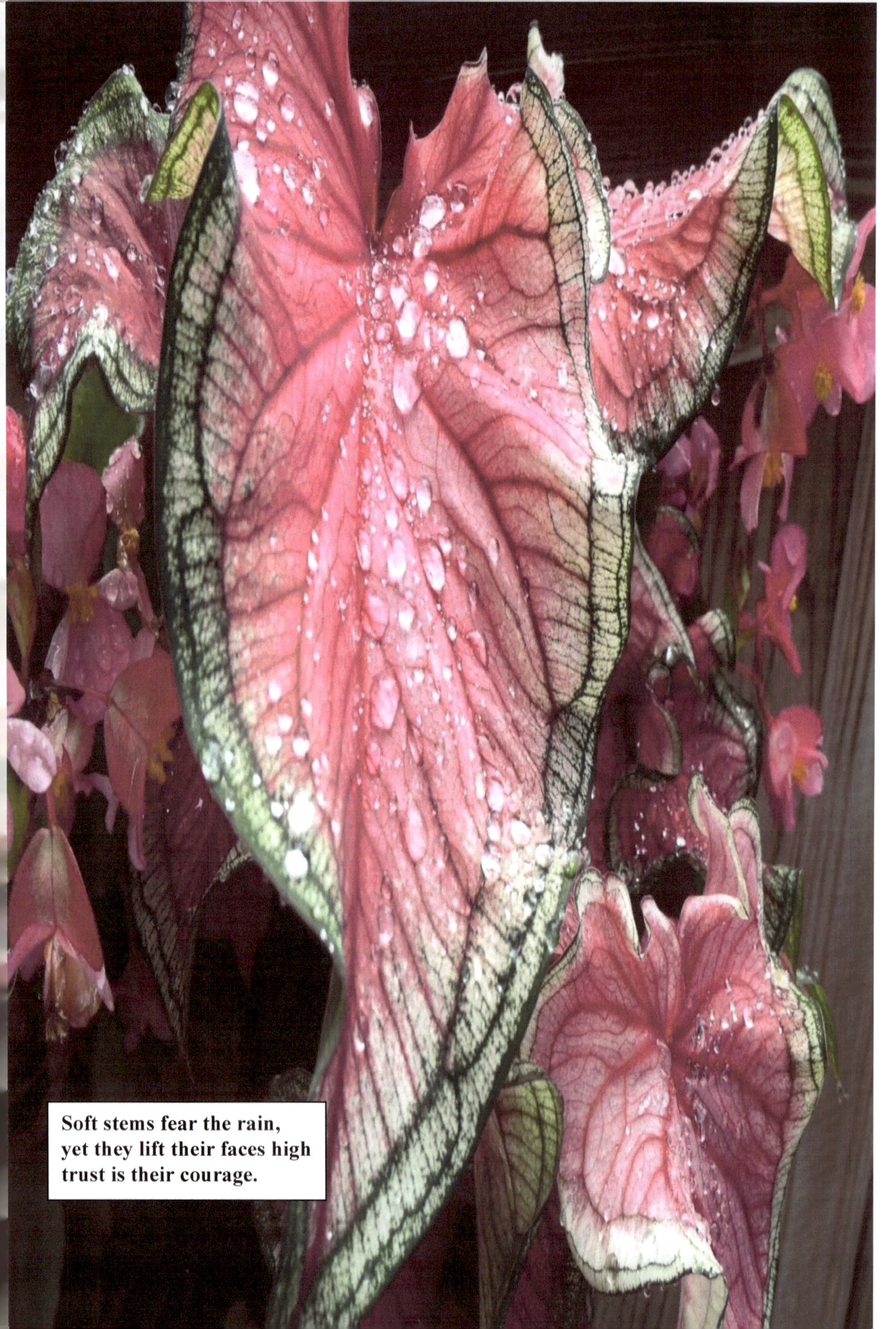
Soft stems fear the rain,
yet they lift their faces high
trust is their courage.

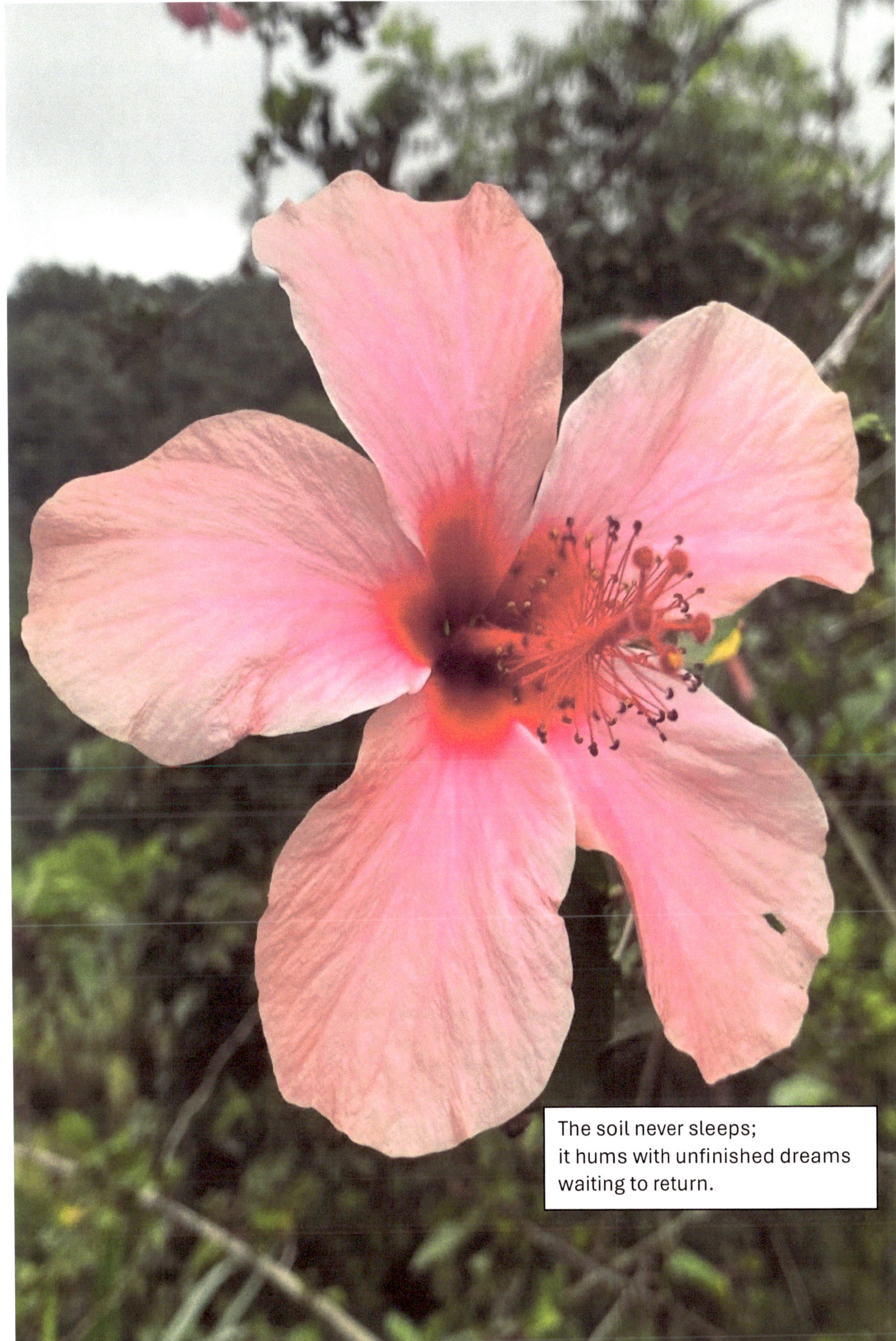
The soil never sleeps;
it hums with unfinished dreams
waiting to return.

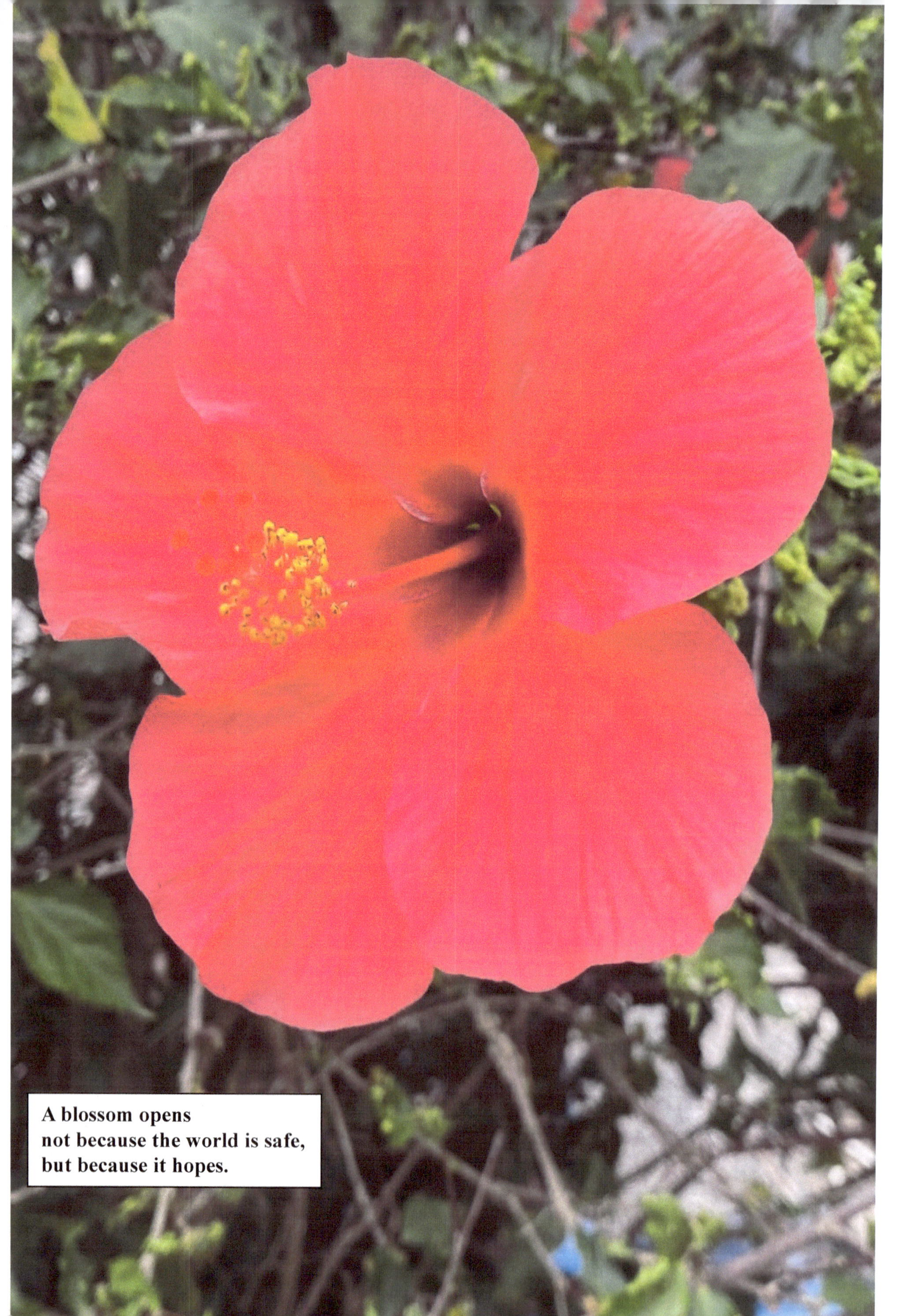
A blossom opens
not because the world is safe,
but because it hopes.

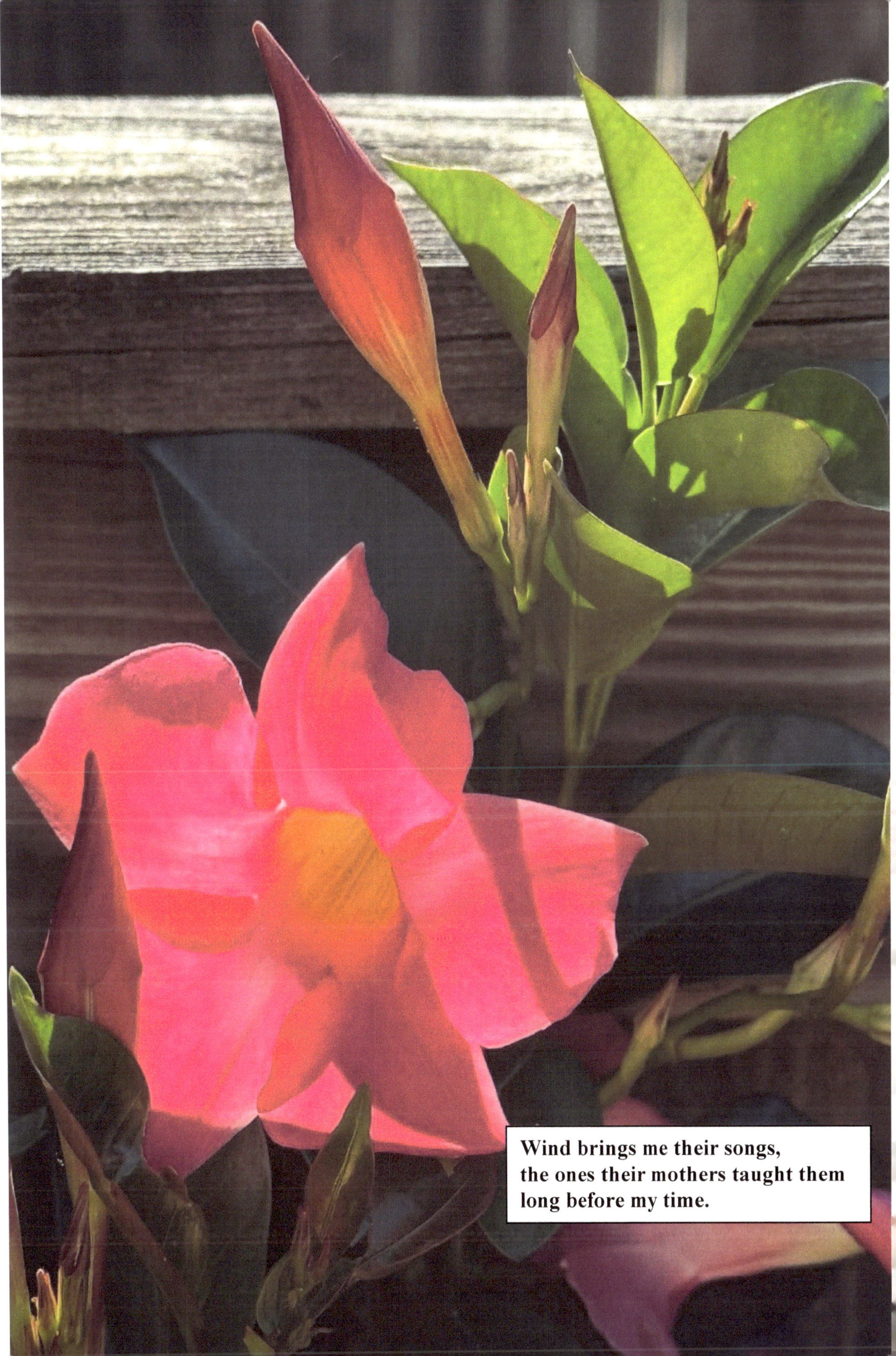
Wind brings me their songs,
the ones their mothers taught them
long before my time.

PART II — WHAT I WITNESSED

I have lived long enough
to watch the world change its mind
over and over again.

Long enough to see the soil rise and sink,
to feel the water table breathe
like a chest that once expanded freely
but now struggles for air.

The flowers do not know these things.
Their lives are brief—
measured in sunlight,
not centuries.

They believe the world has always been
as it is now.
They believe the colors they wear
are the same colors
their ancestors carried.

But I remember otherwise.

I have seen petals shift
from pale to vivid,
from wide to narrow,
from species that sang in harmony
to new ones that hum in unfamiliar keys.
Mutations, they call them—
but to me, they are simply
the earth trying new stories.

Some stories thrive.
Some disappear quietly,
leaving only a memory
that clings to my bark
like a soft fingerprint.

Humans changed too.
I have watched them
arrive with wooden buckets,
then iron tools,
then shiny metal mouths
that tear earth open
with a sound that makes my roots flinch.

And yet—
I have also watched humans kneel.
Kneel with reverence,
pouring water slowly
as if afraid to disturb a single grain of soil.

I have seen them whisper apologies
to a broken stem.
I have seen them rejoice
over a sudden bloom
as if they themselves
had sprouted color overnight.

Humans forget their gentleness
more often than they lose it.
That is the truth I have learned.

The flowers fear humans
because they know only the instant—
only the moment the shears appear,
or the moment a shoe comes too close,
or the moment a hand plucks one of them
before her season is complete.

They shake in the wind,
asking me why.
Always asking why.

I tell them,
"Humans are born with storms inside.
But many carry rain too—

rain that nourishes,
rain that remembers how to fall softly."

I have seen centuries of that rain.
Kindness passed through hands
that plant new hope in the ground.

And I have seen storms—
the kind that do not come from the sky
but from human impatience,
human noise,
human wanting.

I remember the first drought—
the one that cracked the soil
like ancient pottery.
Water ran shallow that year,
and my leaves grew thin
from carrying the weight
of trying to shield too many
and save too few.

The flowers did not understand.
They wilted with questions
I could not answer.

But then another kind of rain came.
Humans touched the earth with care,
bringing buckets of water
as if delivering something holy.
The flowers lifted their heads
as though waking from a dream
they did not want to remember.

I have seen soil dry
and soil healed.
I have seen roots pulled
and roots reborn.

I once watched humans
replant an entire corner of the garden
after a disease swept through it.
The flowers who bloom there now
have no idea
how much grief the ground endured
before they arrived.

But I know.
I felt it.
The soil still sighs sometimes
with that memory.

There were years
when the rain came too hard,
flooding the garden
and drowning tender seedlings
before they learned to stand.
I tried to hold back the storm,
spreading my limbs wide
as if I could push back the sky.
But even I
cannot command the weather.

The flowers forgave me
for the ones washed away.
They always forgive.
Perhaps that is why
they return even after the harshest season—
their trust is inherited
the way light is inherited by dawn.

I have witnessed
the rise and fall
of more lives than I can count.
I have seen beauty perish
and beauty resurrect
in shapes familiar and strange.

And through it all,
the flowers have believed
I am their God.

But I have never been more
than a patient witness
who refuses to walk away.

Turn these pages
and look closely at what I have seen—
for the flowers' stories are brief,
but mine is long,
and I am trying
to tell it whole.

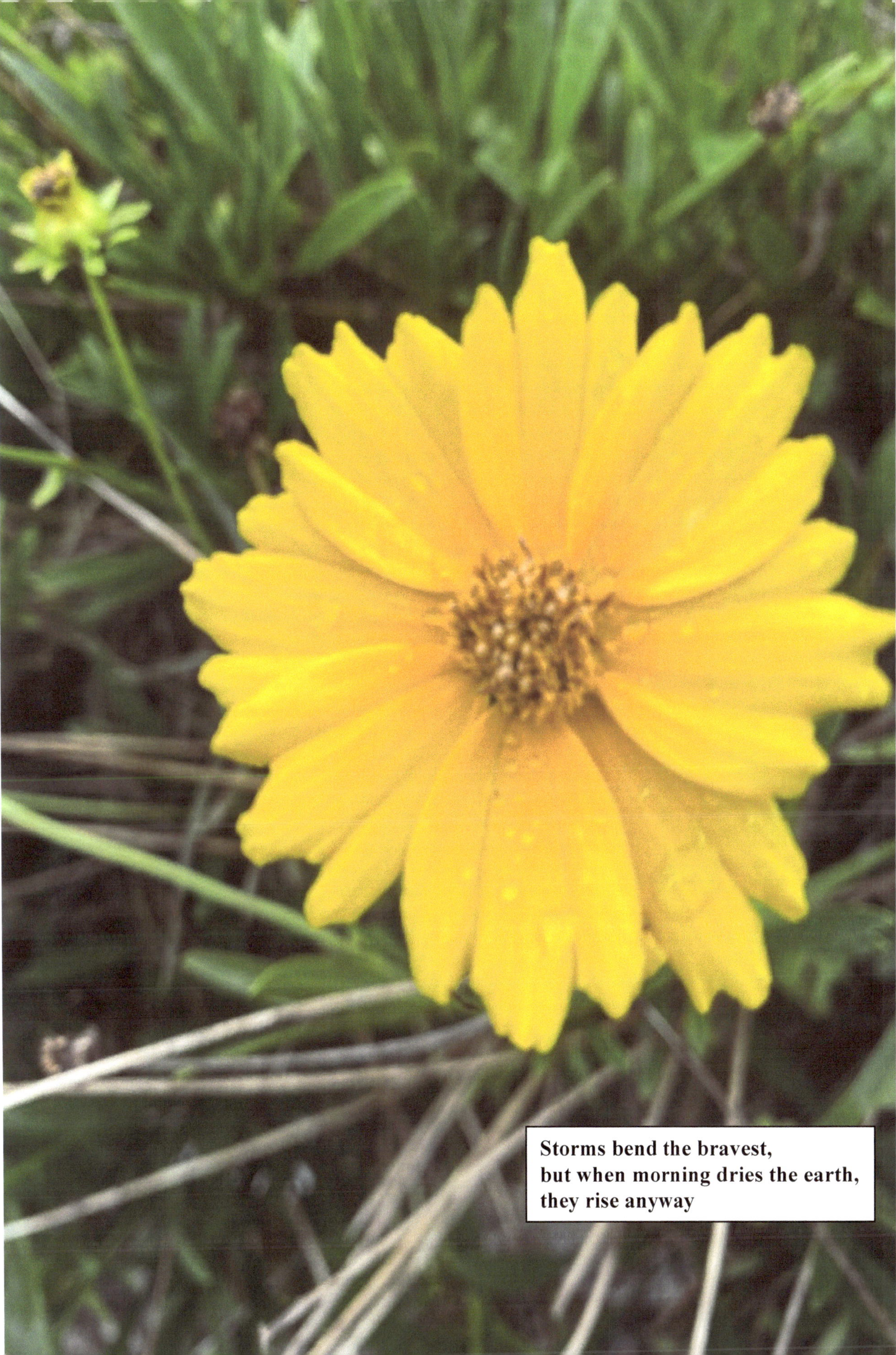
Storms bend the bravest,
but when morning dries the earth,
they rise anyway

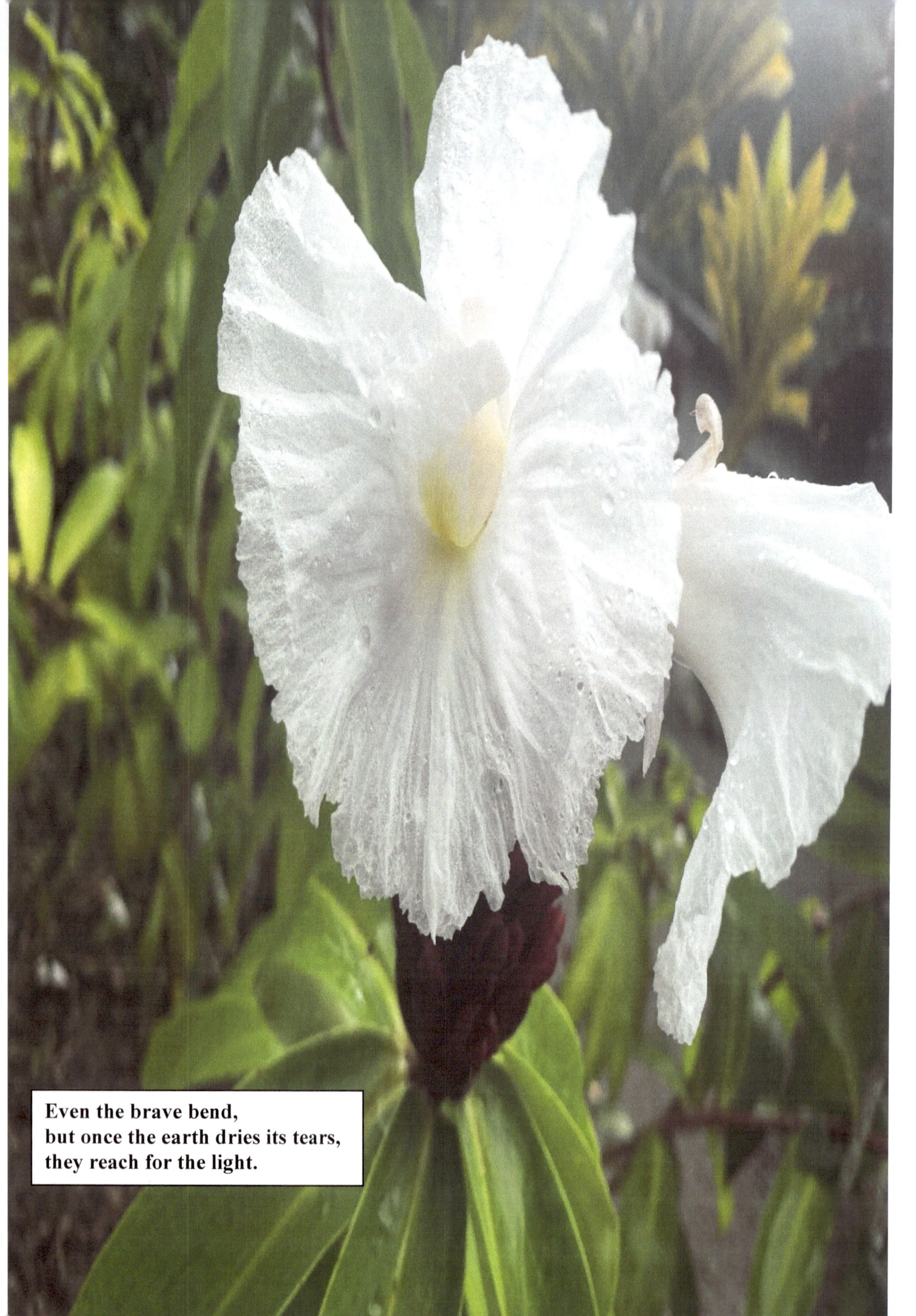
Even the brave bend,
but once the earth dries its tears,
they reach for the light.

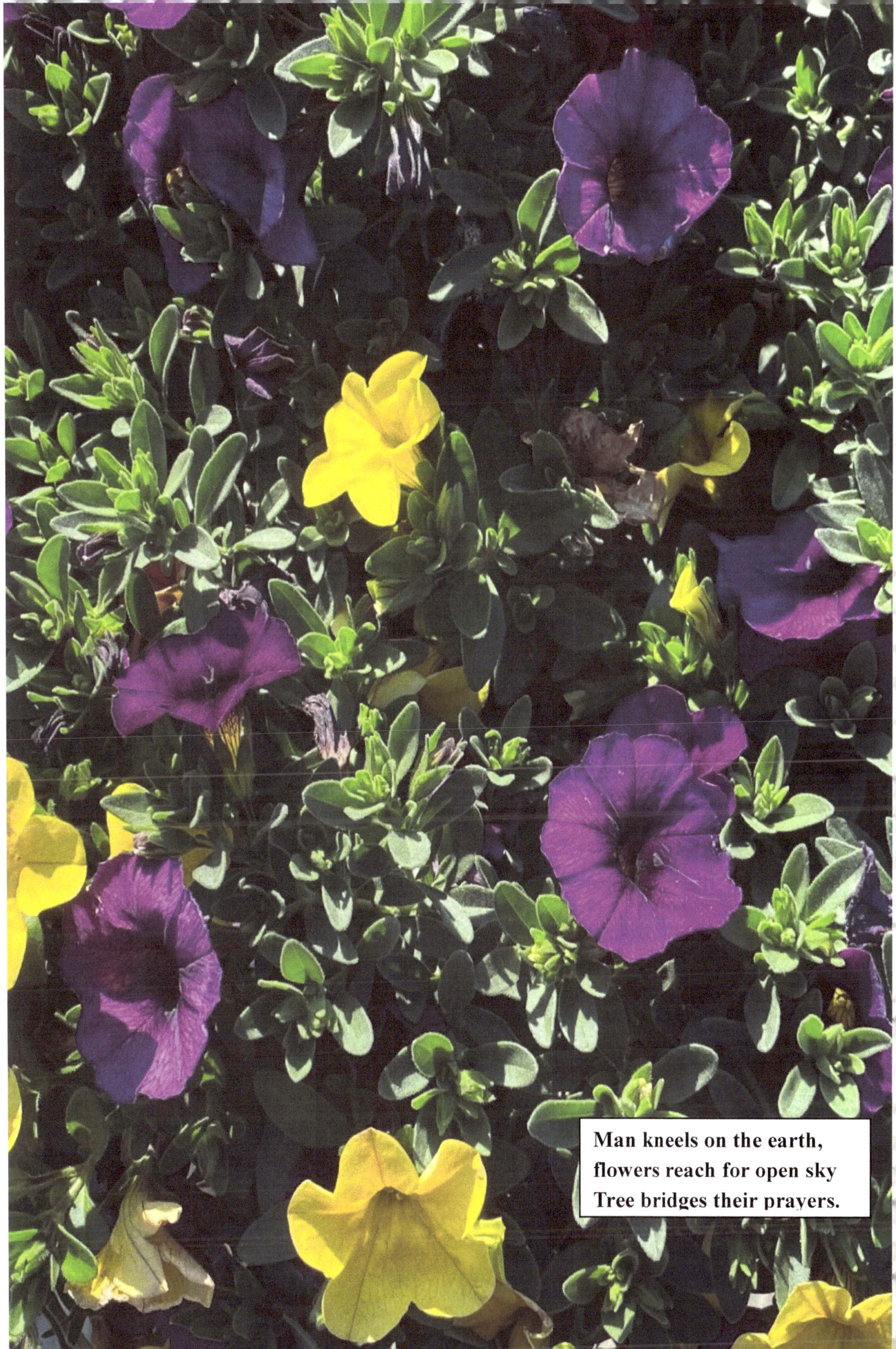

Man kneels on the earth,
flowers reach for open sky
Tree bridges their prayers.

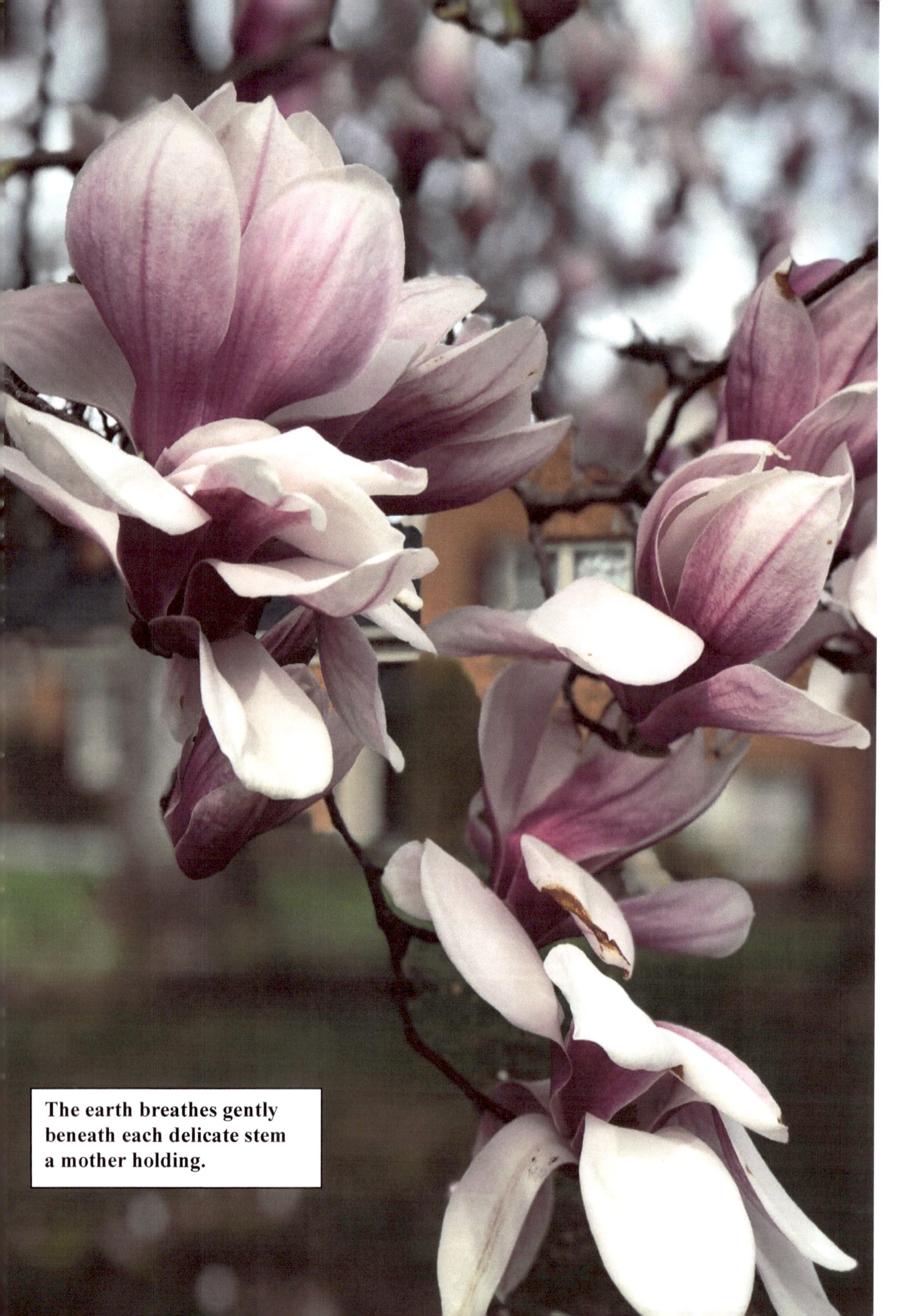

The earth breathes gently
beneath each delicate stem
a mother holding.

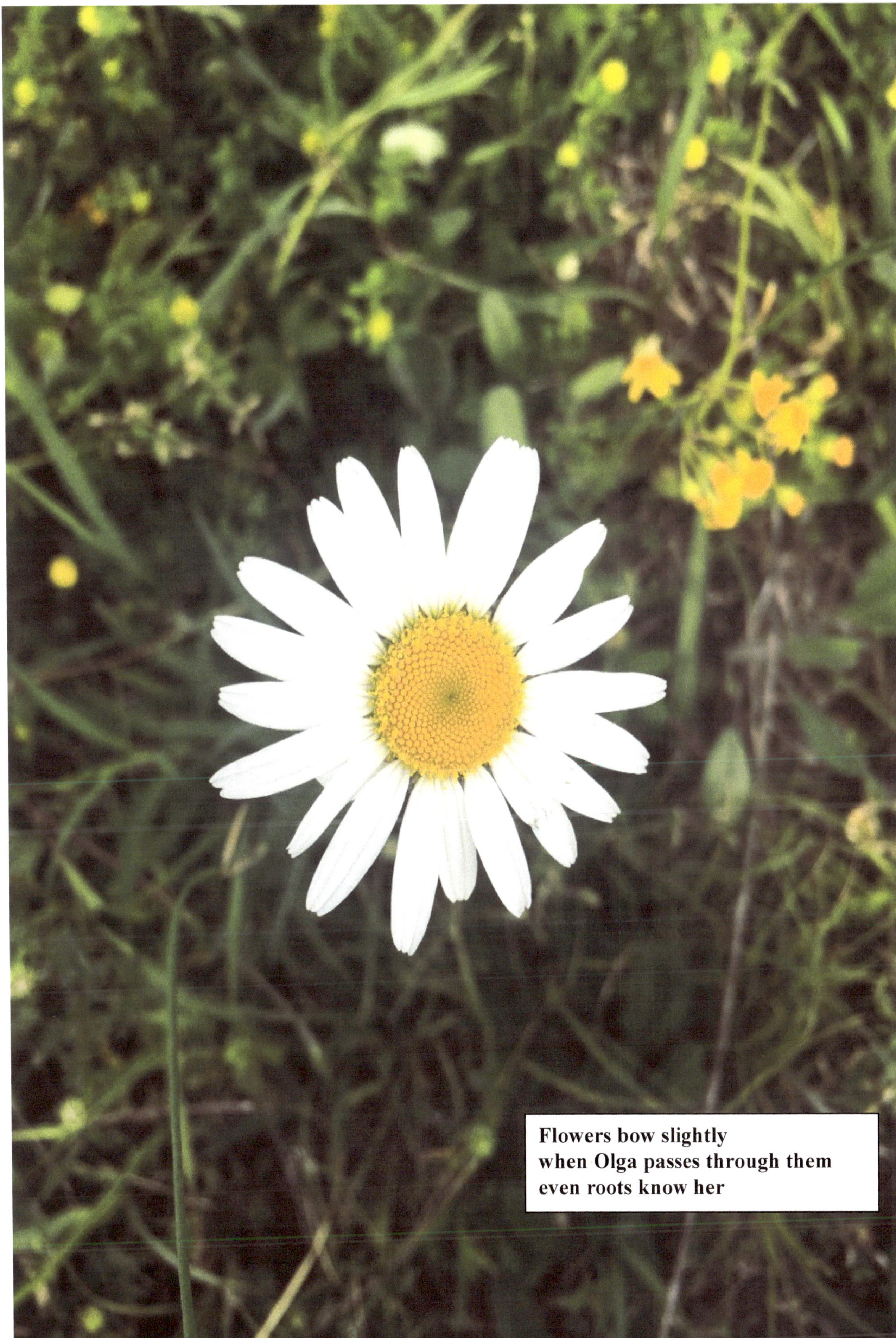
Flowers bow slightly
when Olga passes through them
even roots know her

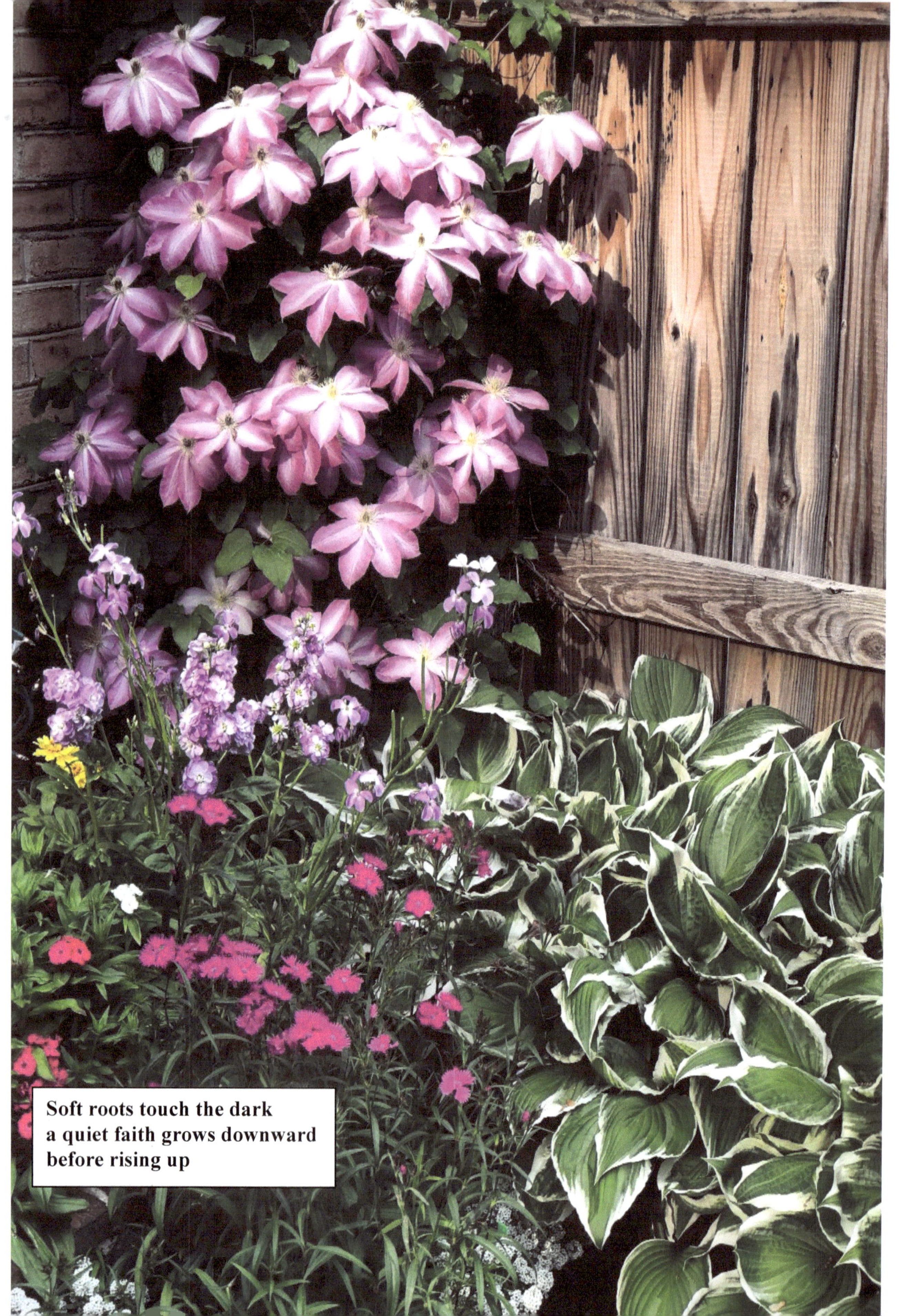
Soft roots touch the dark
a quiet faith grows downward
before rising up

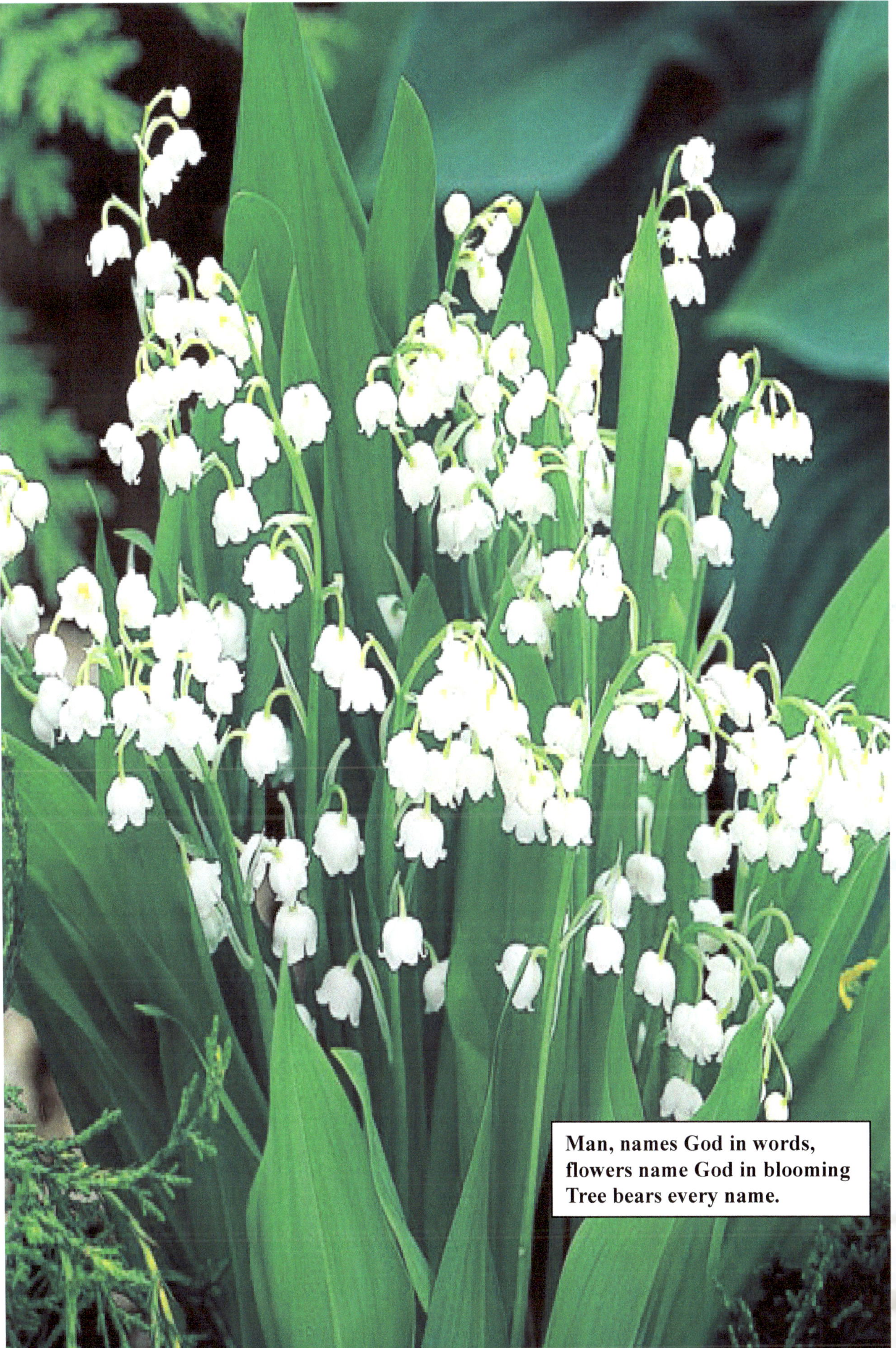
Man, names God in words,
flowers name God in blooming
Tree bears every name.

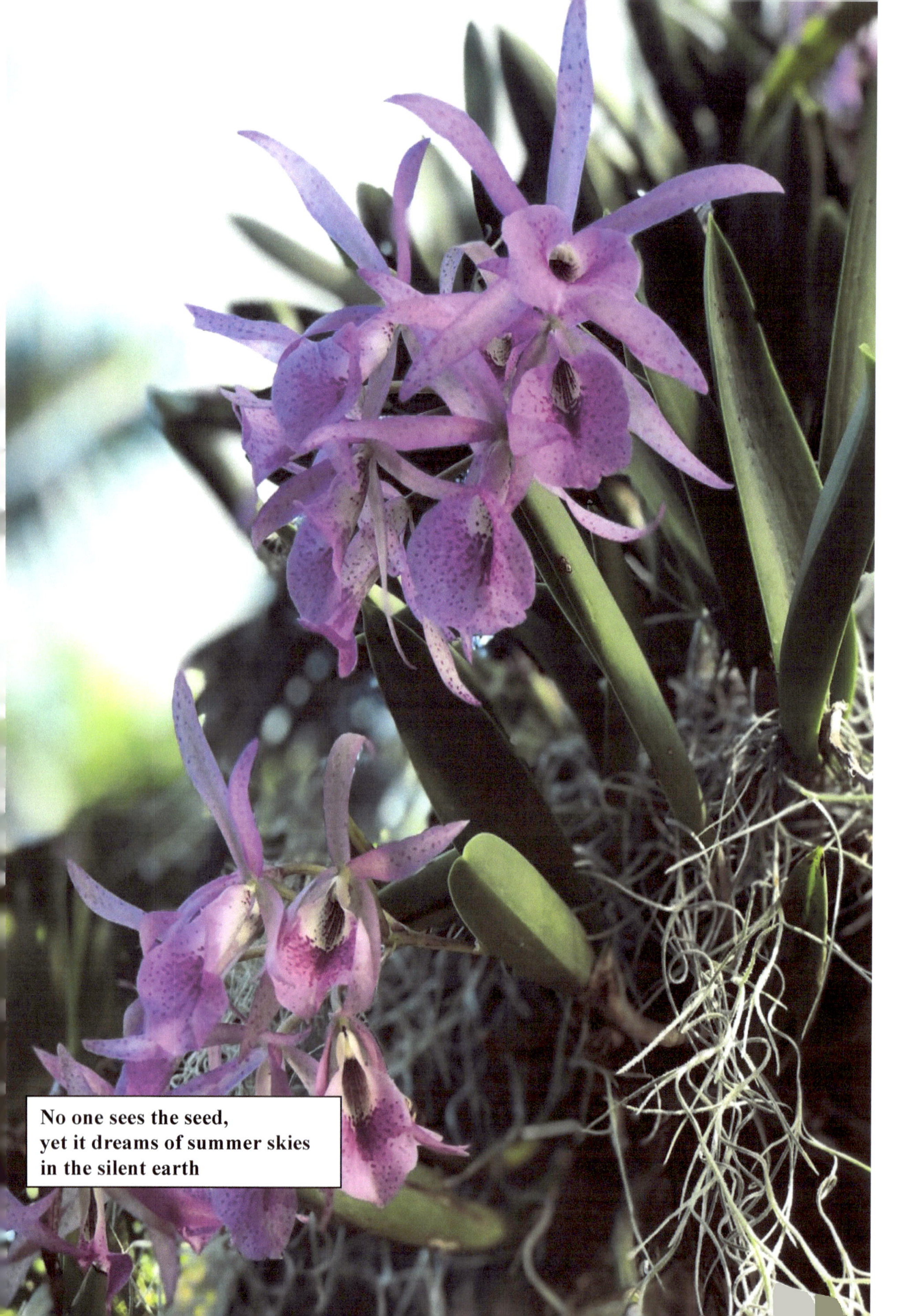
No one sees the seed,
yet it dreams of summer skies
in the silent earth

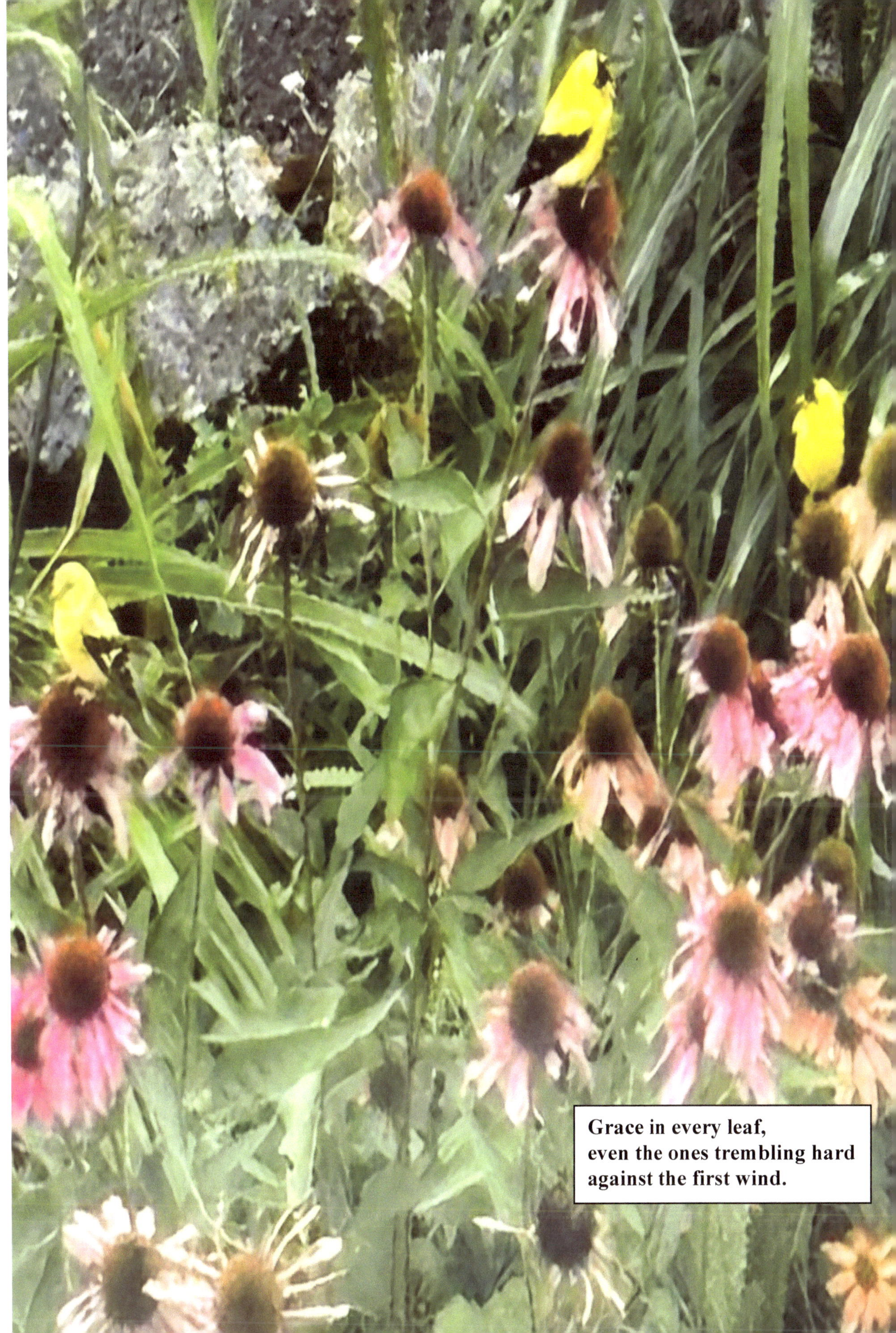

Grace in every leaf,
even the ones trembling hard
against the first wind.

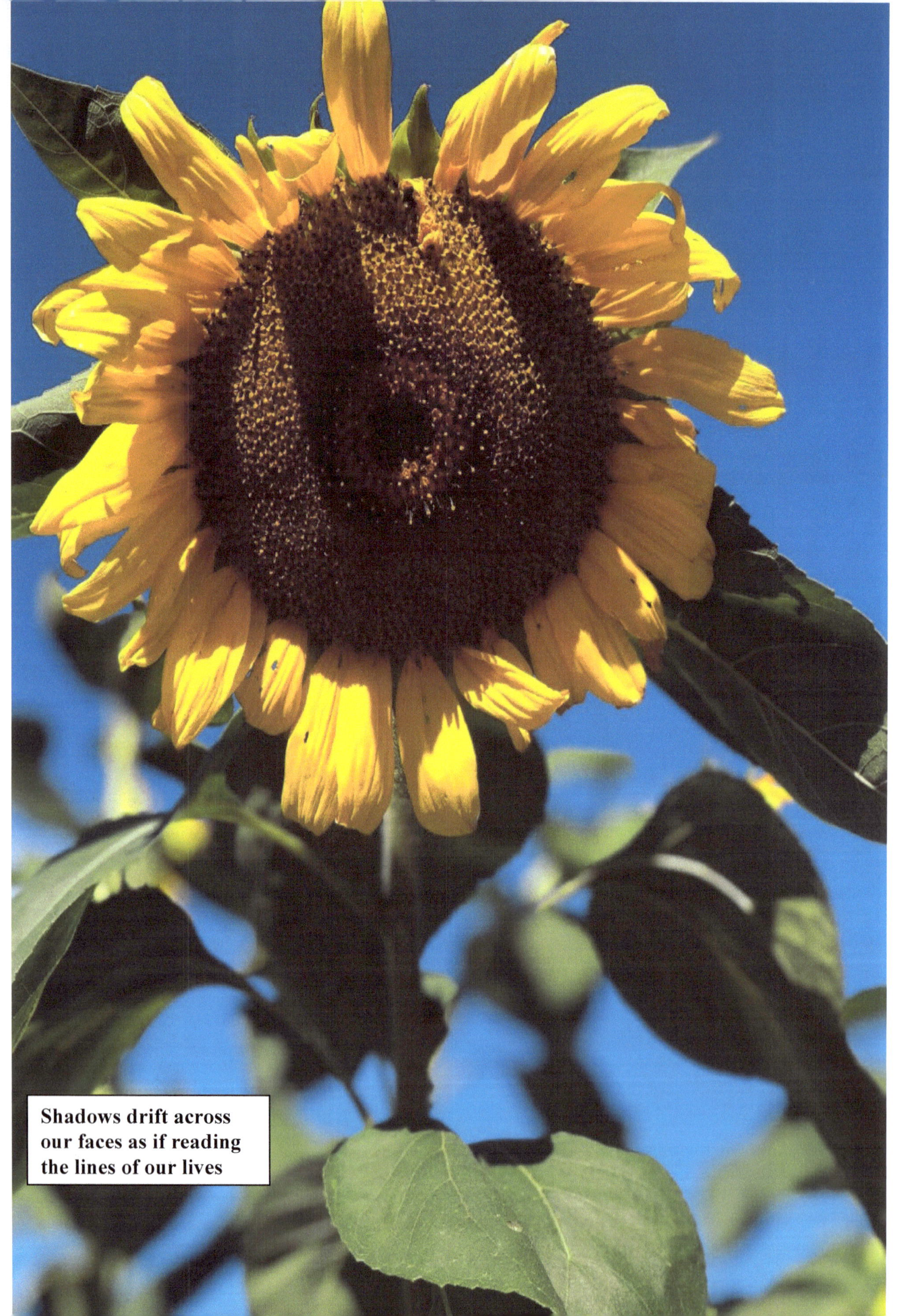

Shadows drift across
our faces as if reading
the lines of our lives

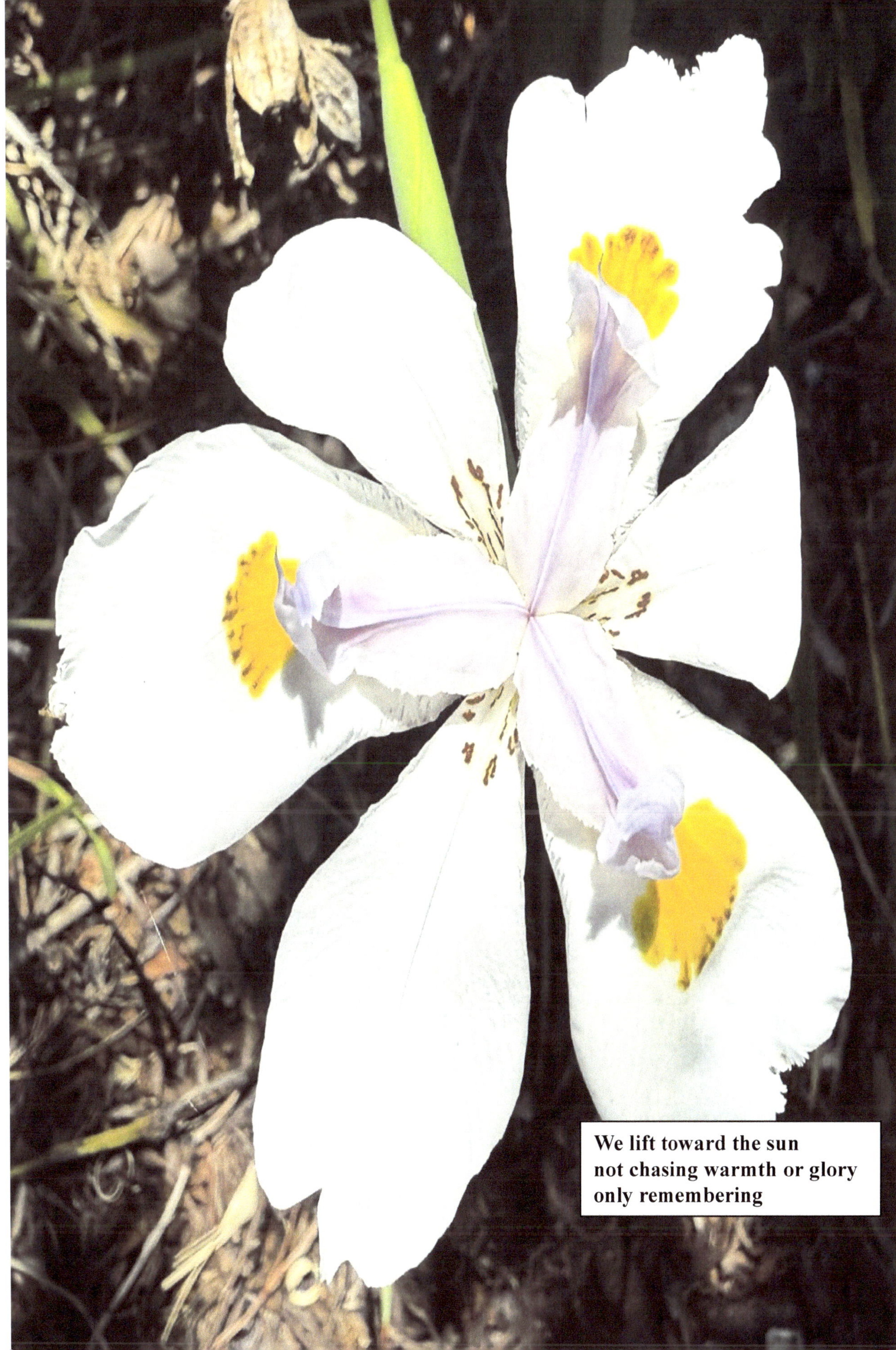
We lift toward the sun
not chasing warmth or glory
only remembering

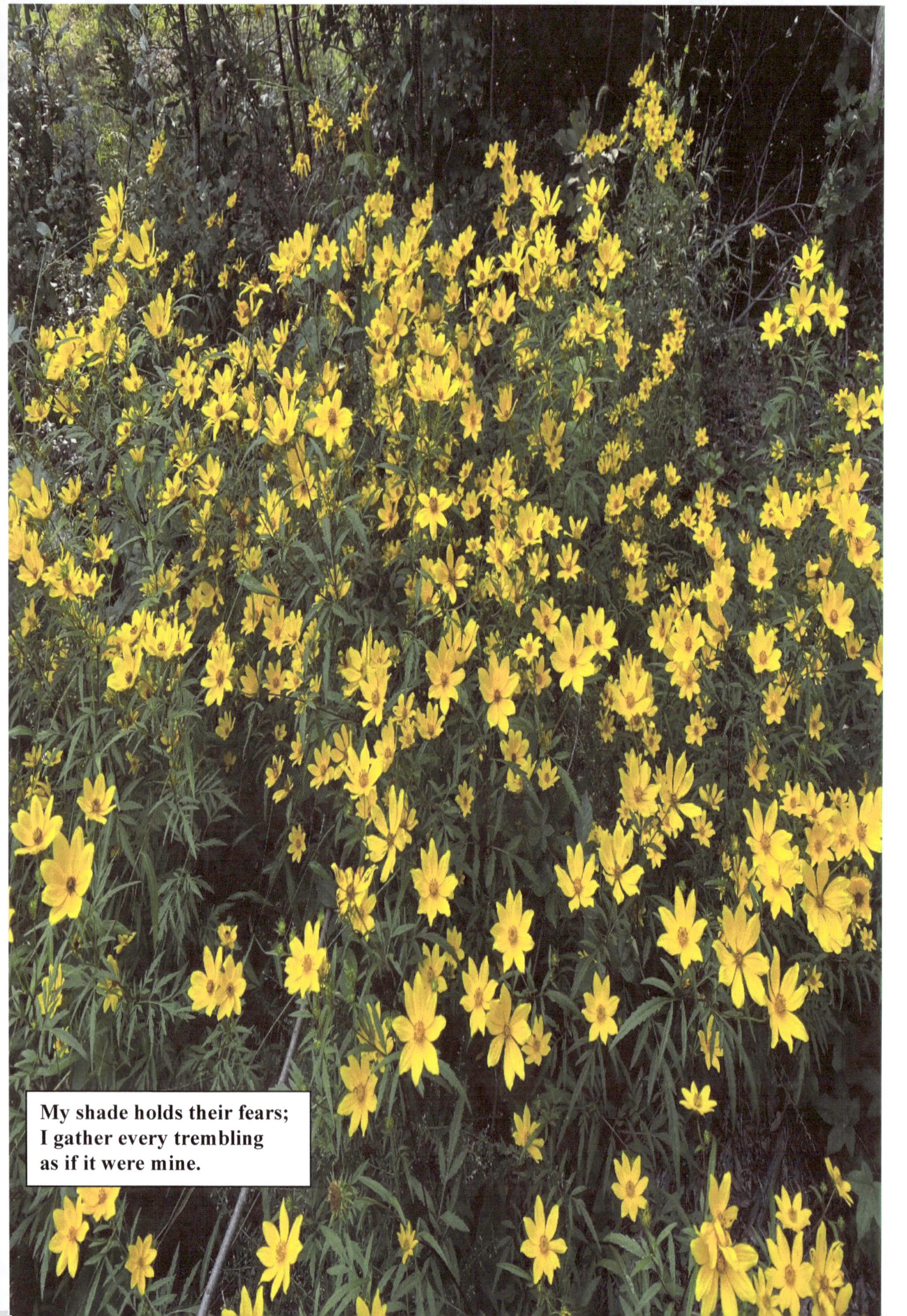
My shade holds their fears;
I gather every trembling
as if it were mine.

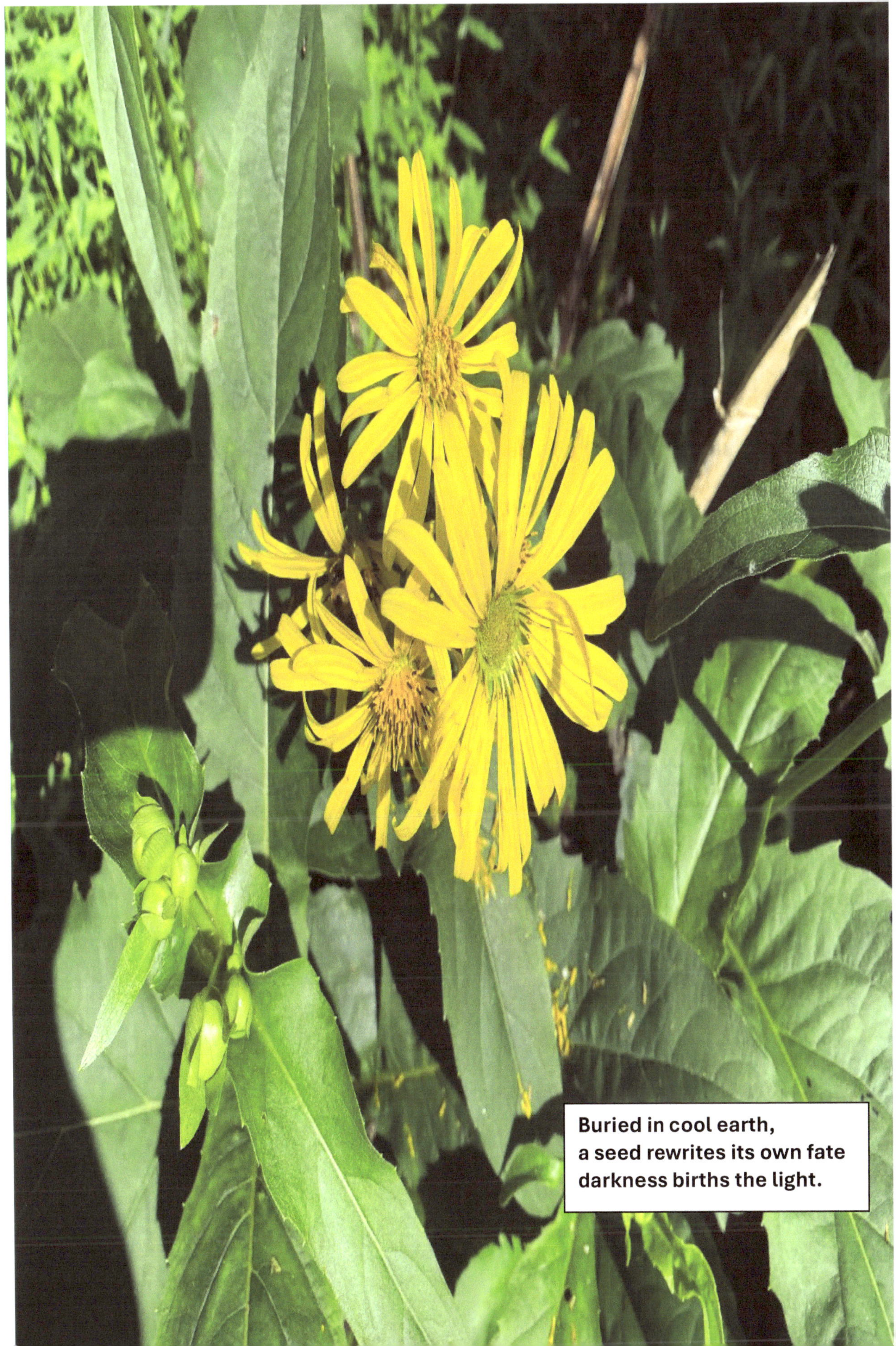
Buried in cool earth,
a seed rewrites its own fate
darkness births the light.

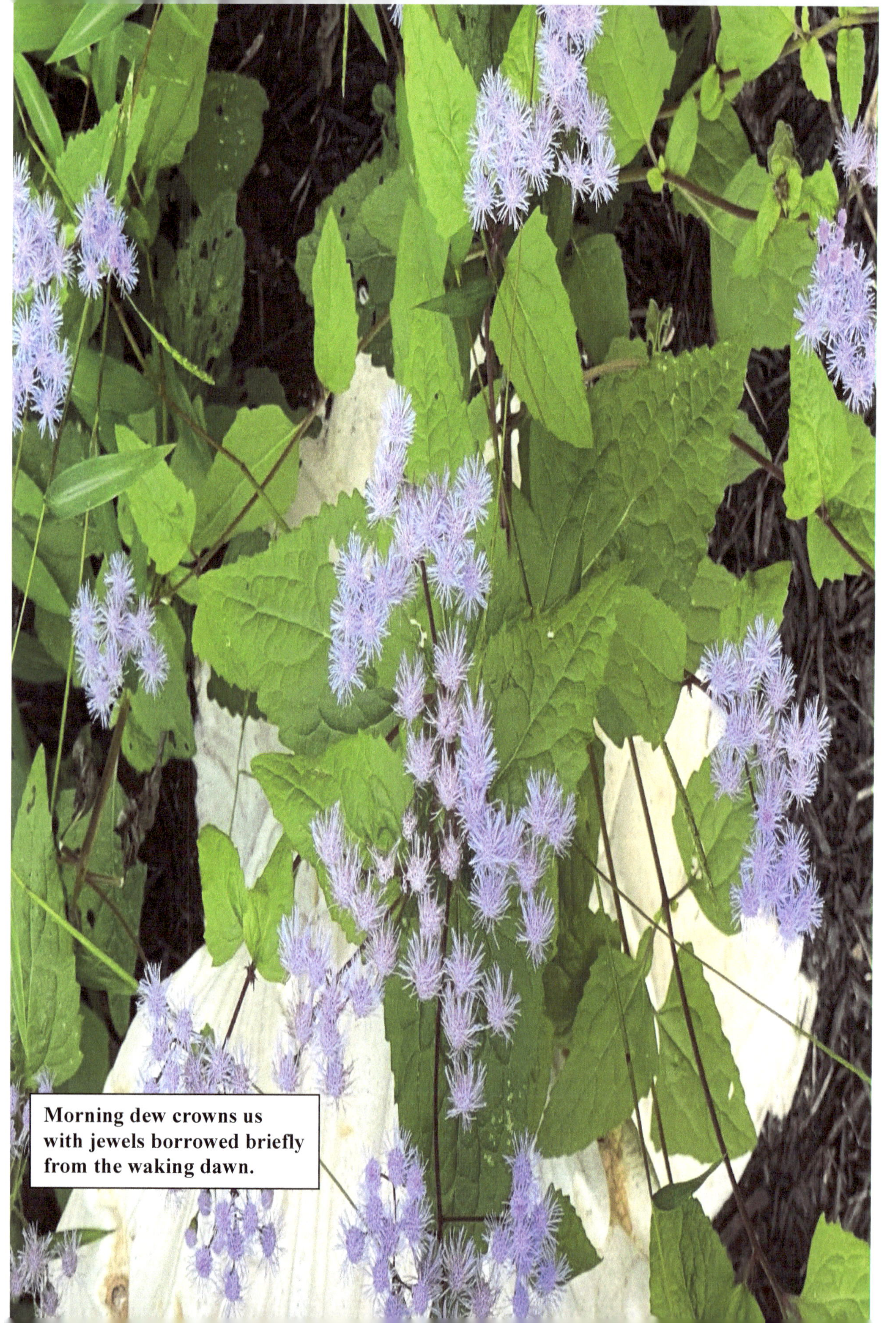

Morning dew crowns us
with jewels borrowed briefly
from the waking dawn.

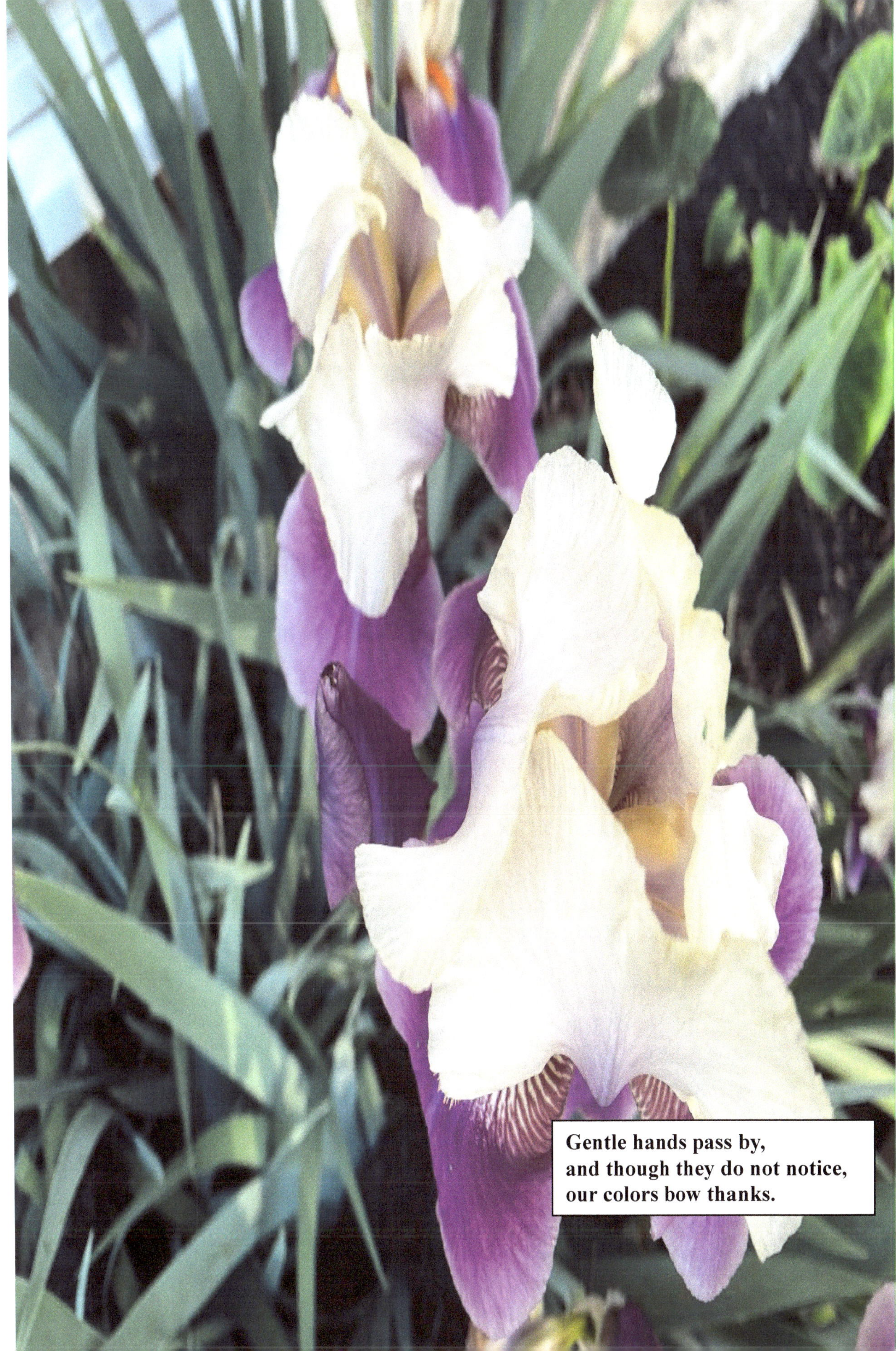
Gentle hands pass by,
and though they do not notice,
our colors bow thanks.

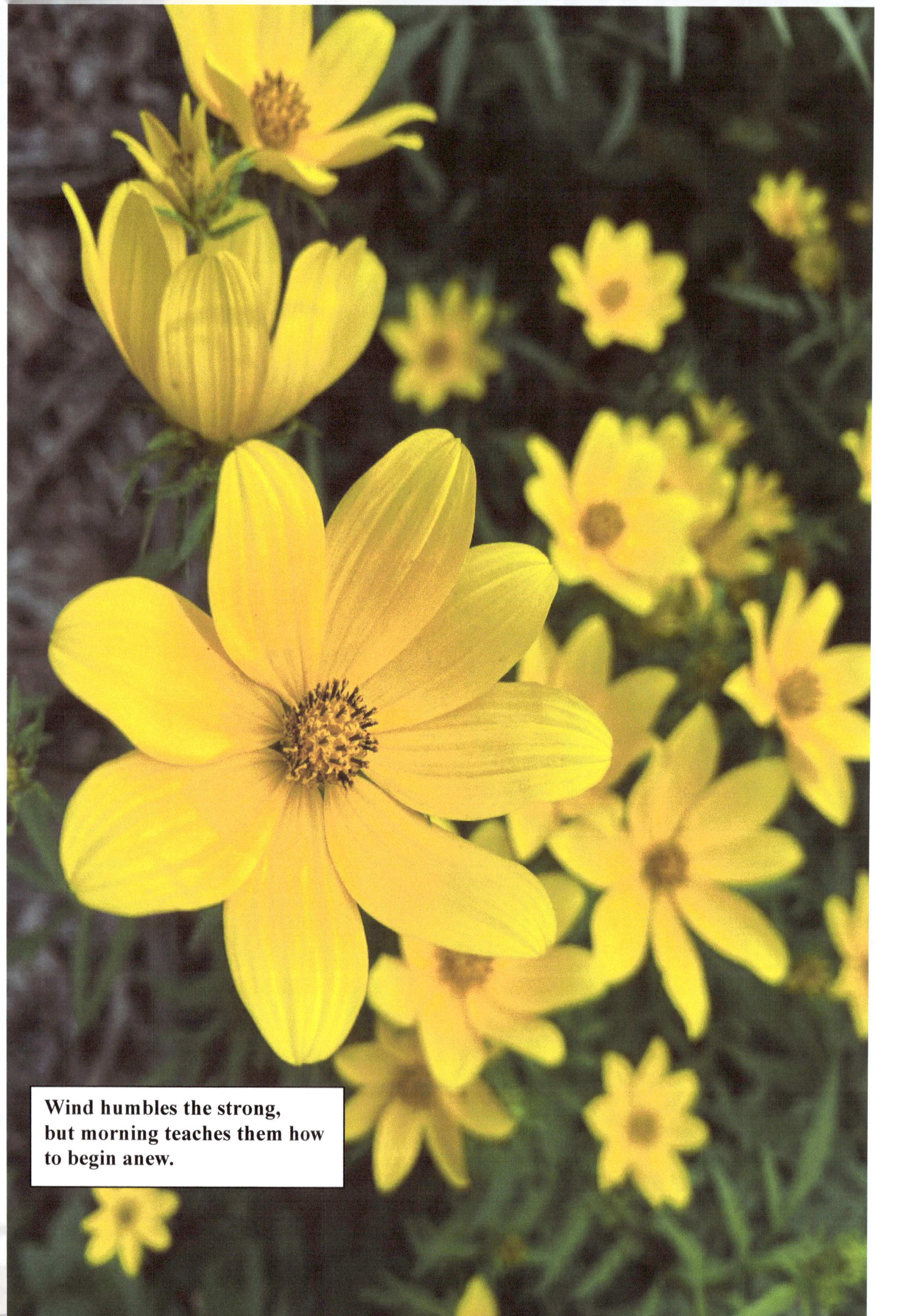
Wind humbles the strong,
but morning teaches them how
to begin anew.

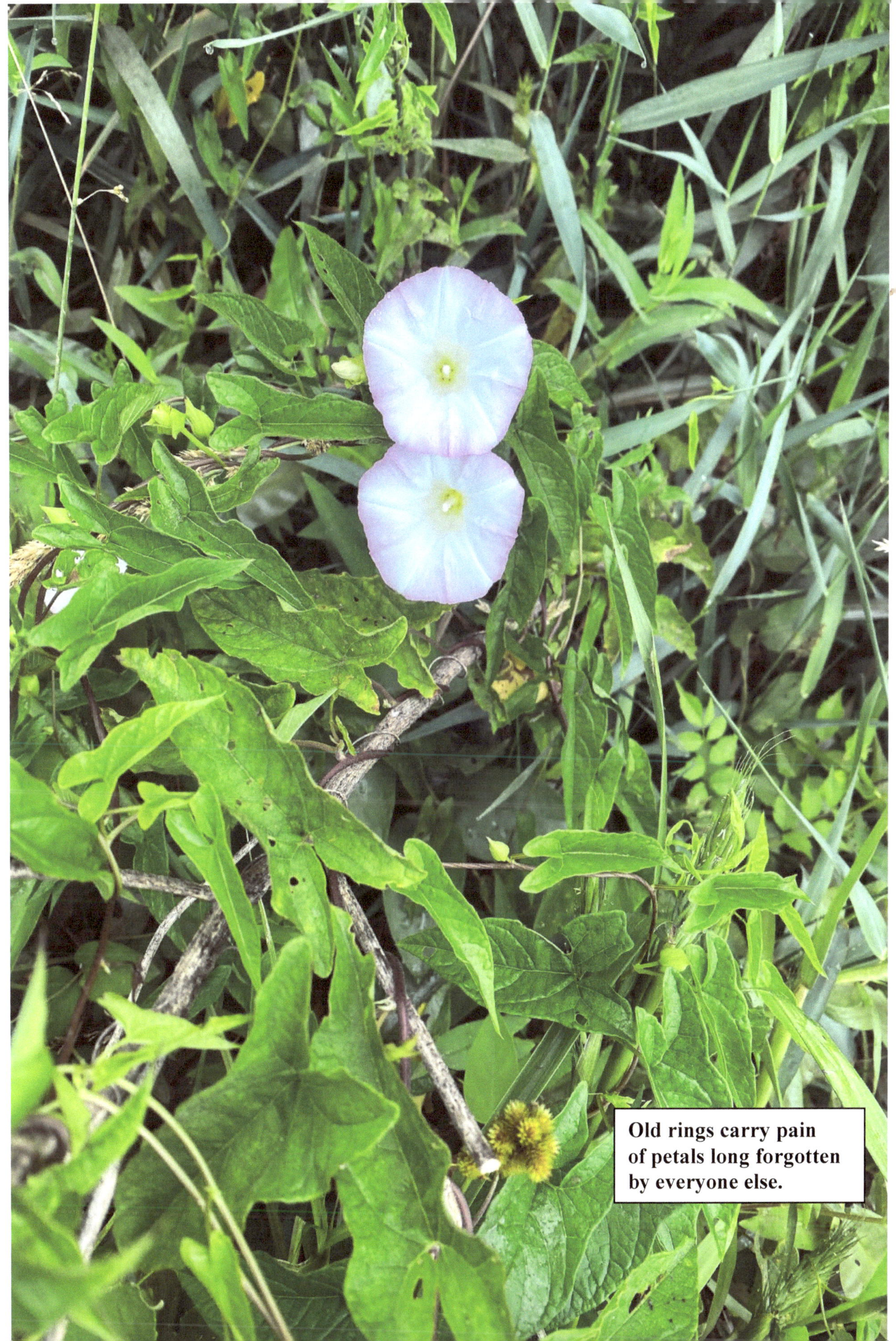
Old rings carry pain
of petals long forgotten
by everyone else.

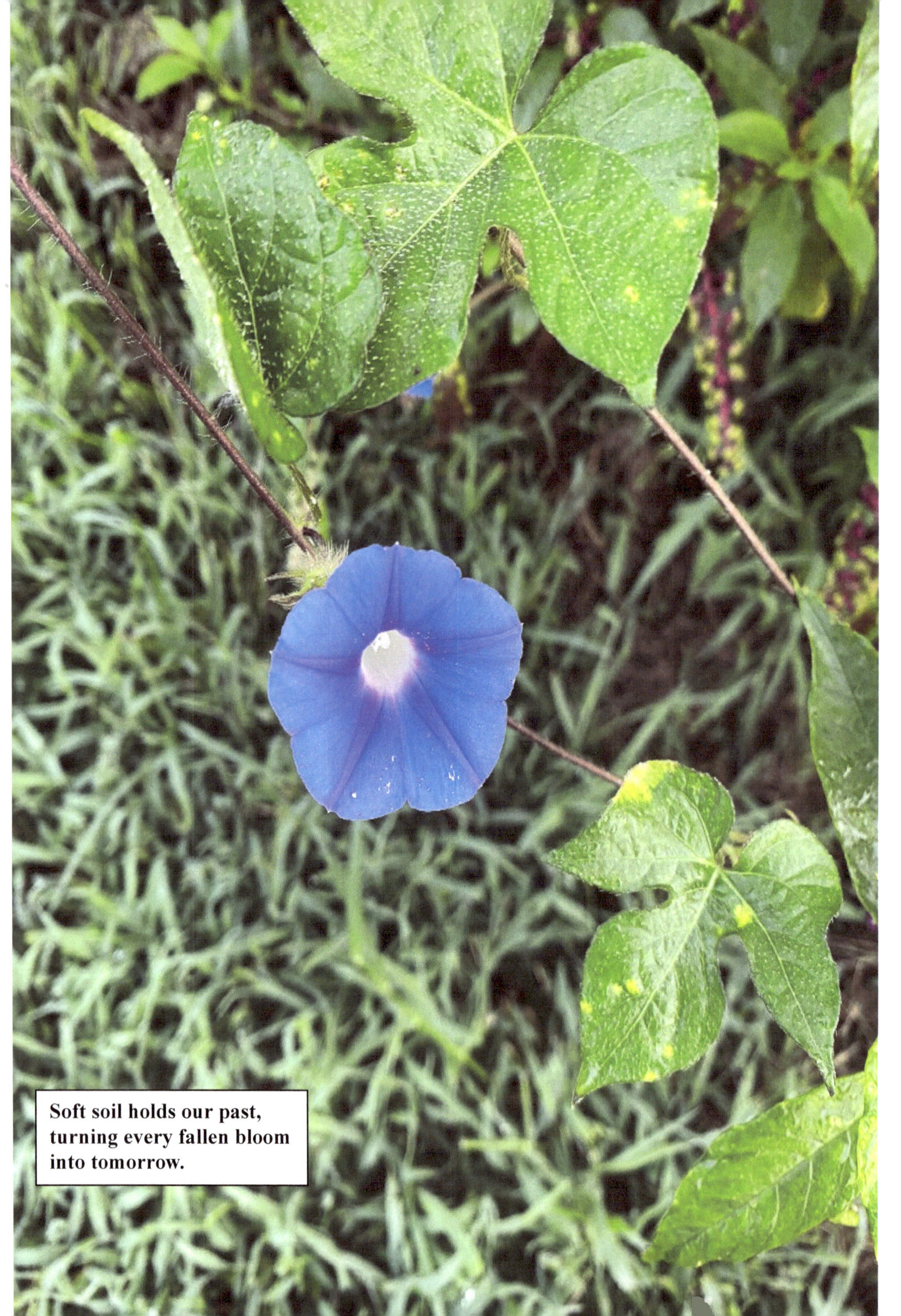
Soft soil holds our past,
turning every fallen bloom
into tomorrow.

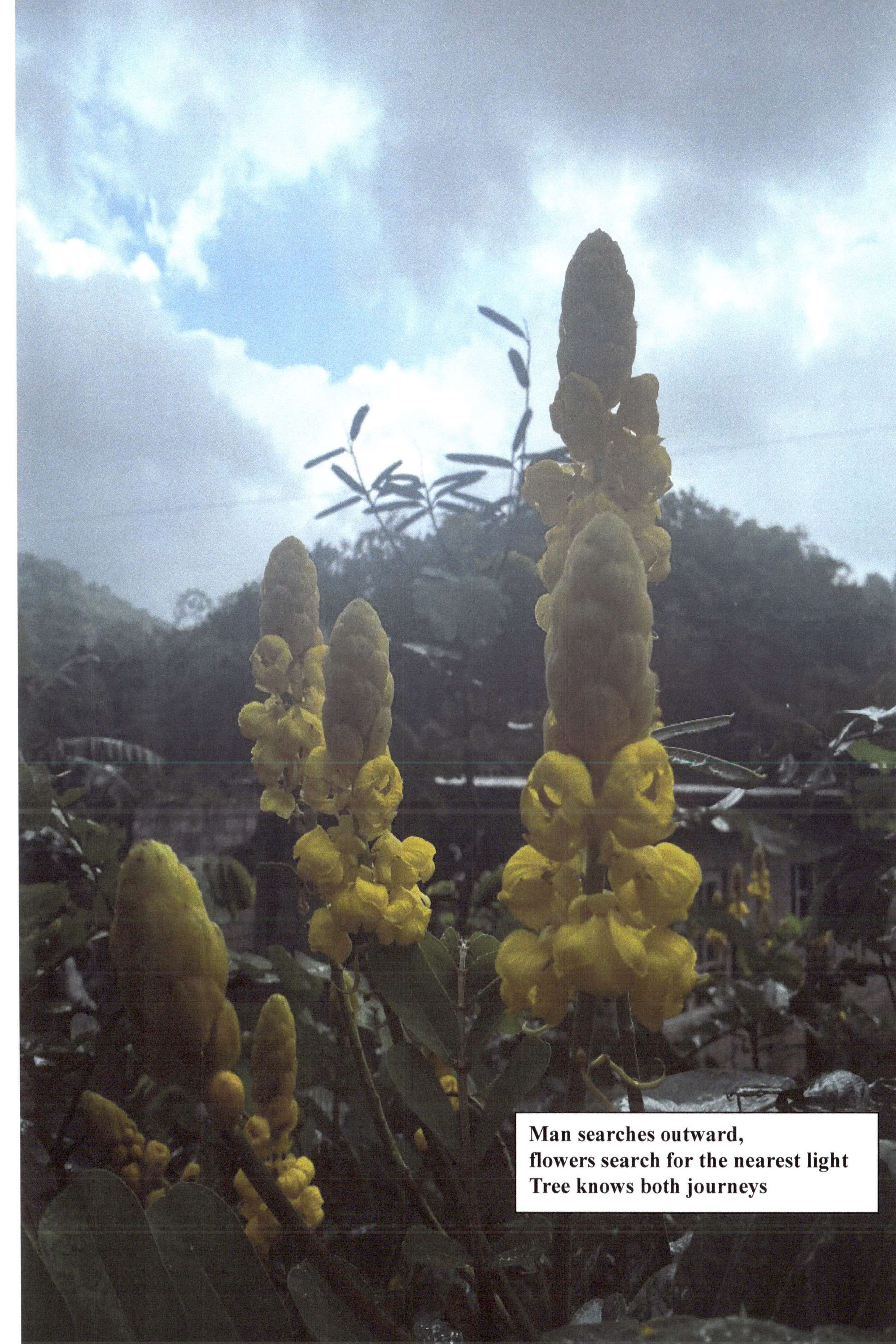
Man searches outward,
flowers search for the nearest light
Tree knows both journeys

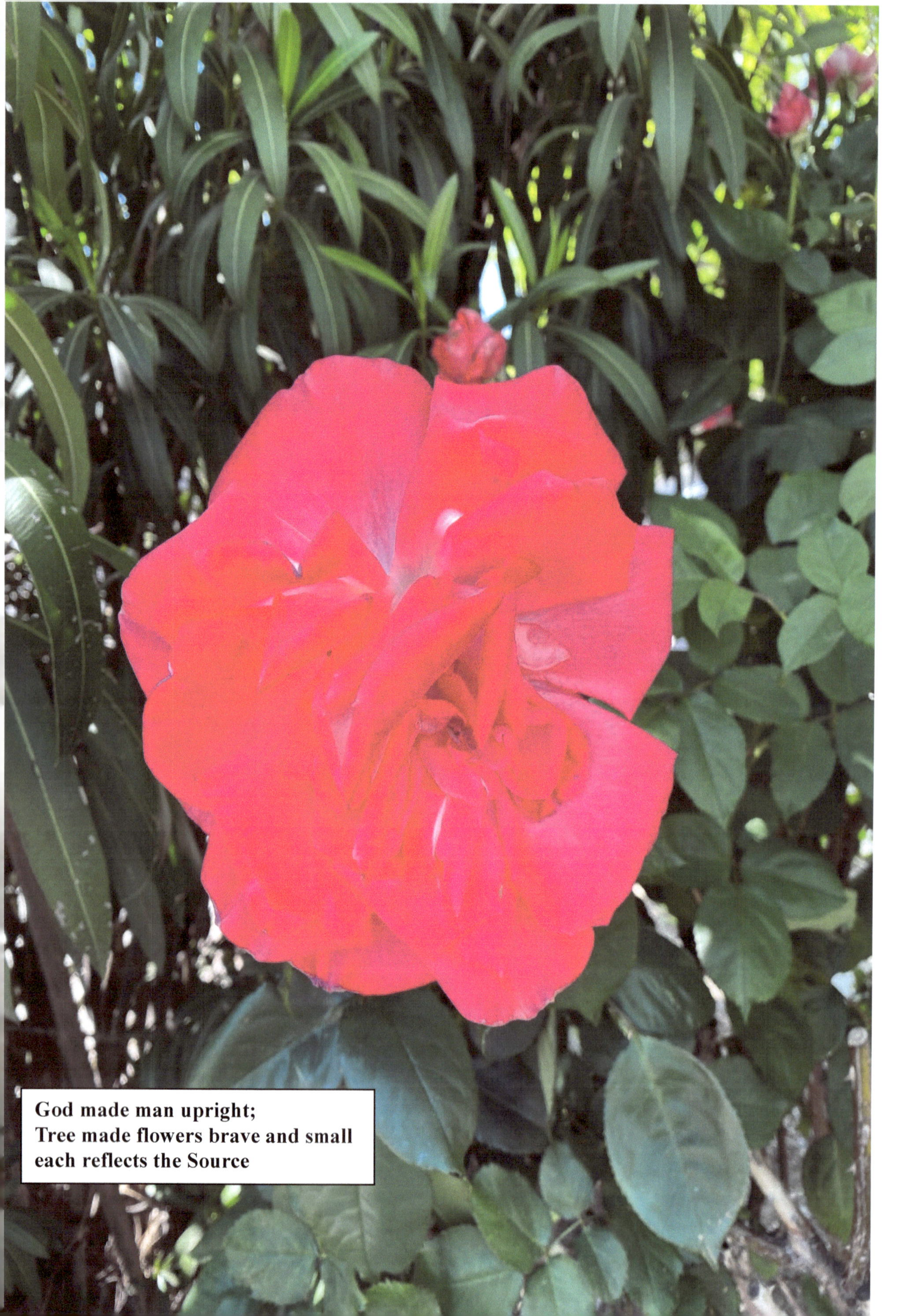
God made man upright;
Tree made flowers brave and small
each reflects the Source

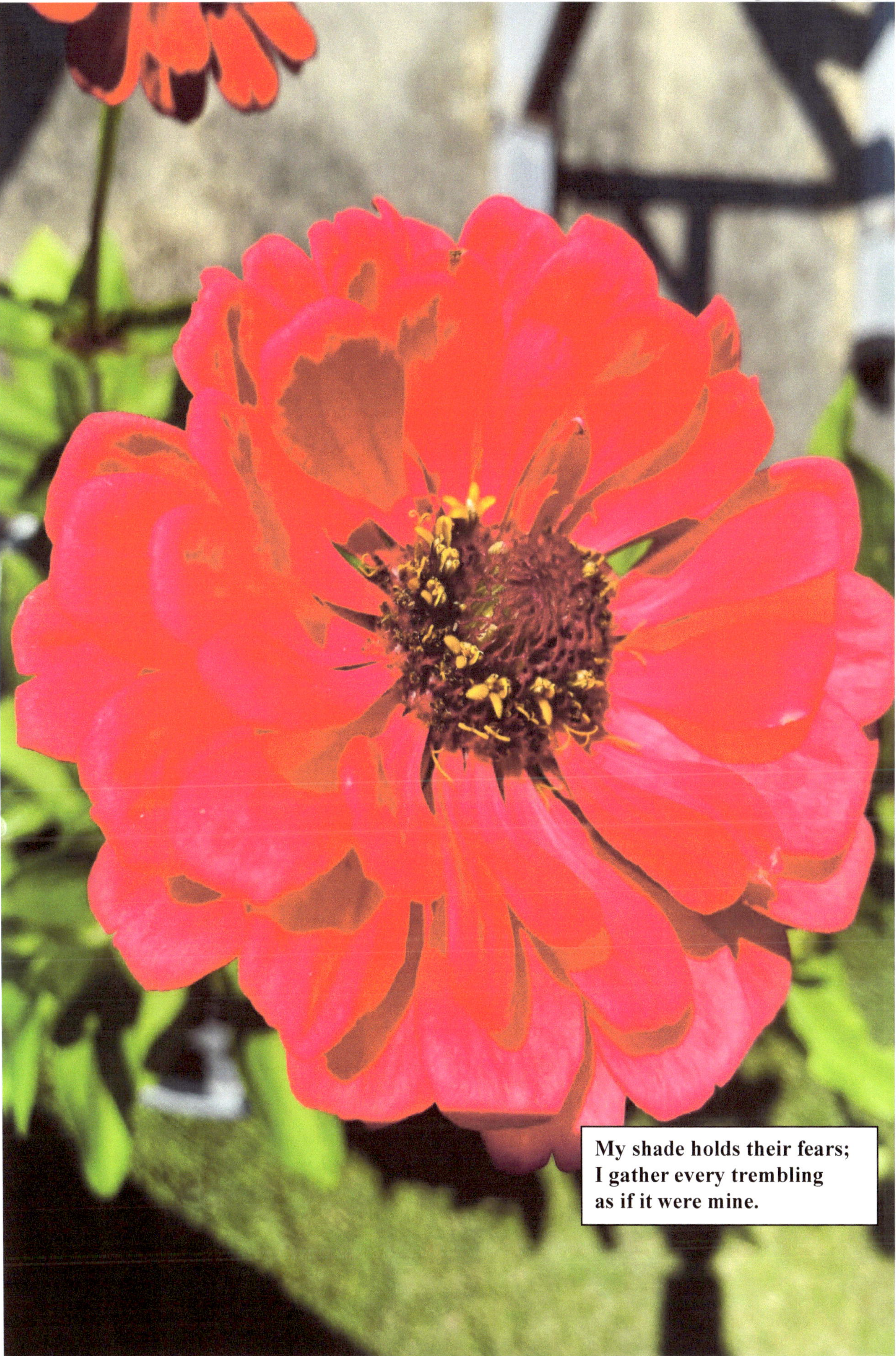
My shade holds their fears;
I gather every trembling
as if it were mine.

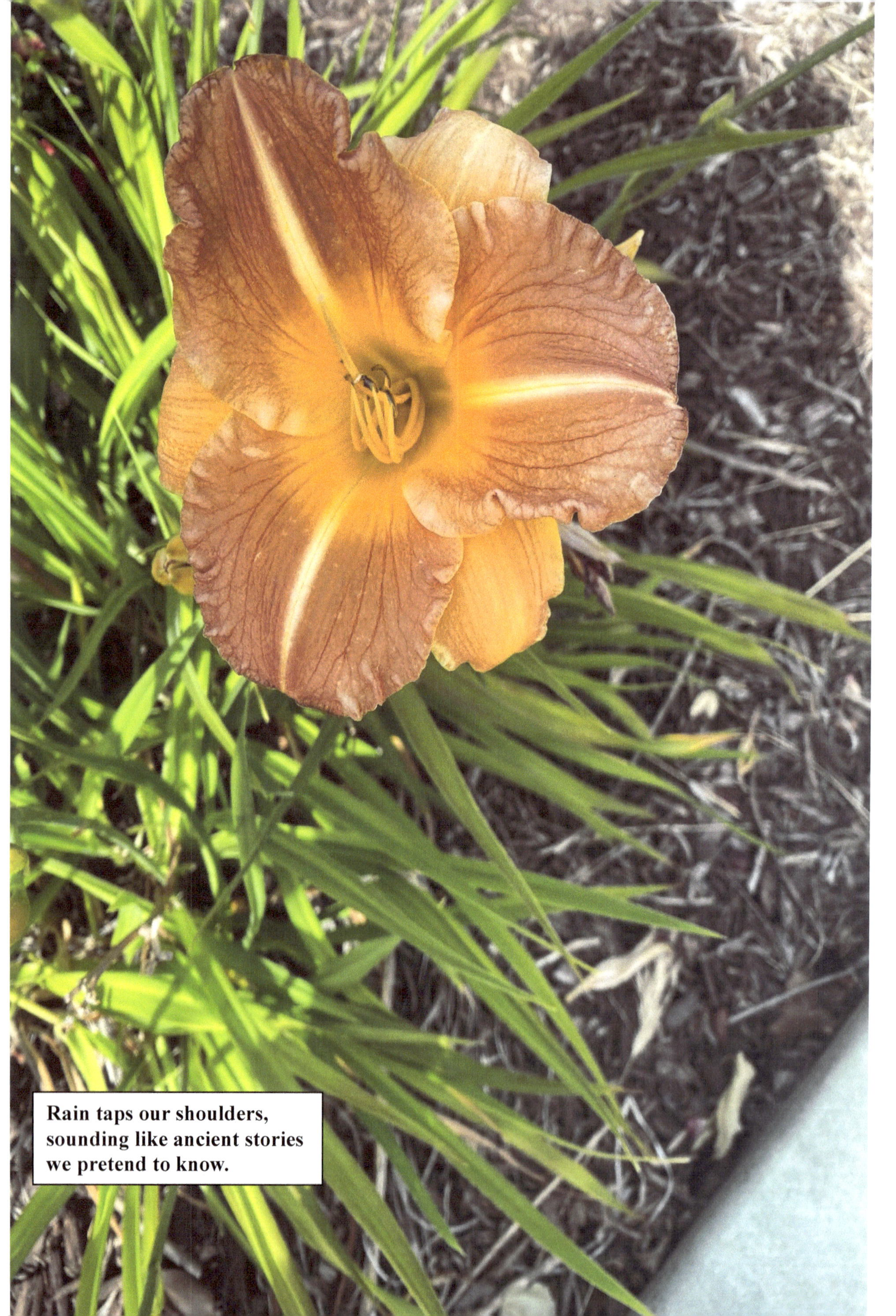
Rain taps our shoulders,
sounding like ancient stories
we pretend to know.

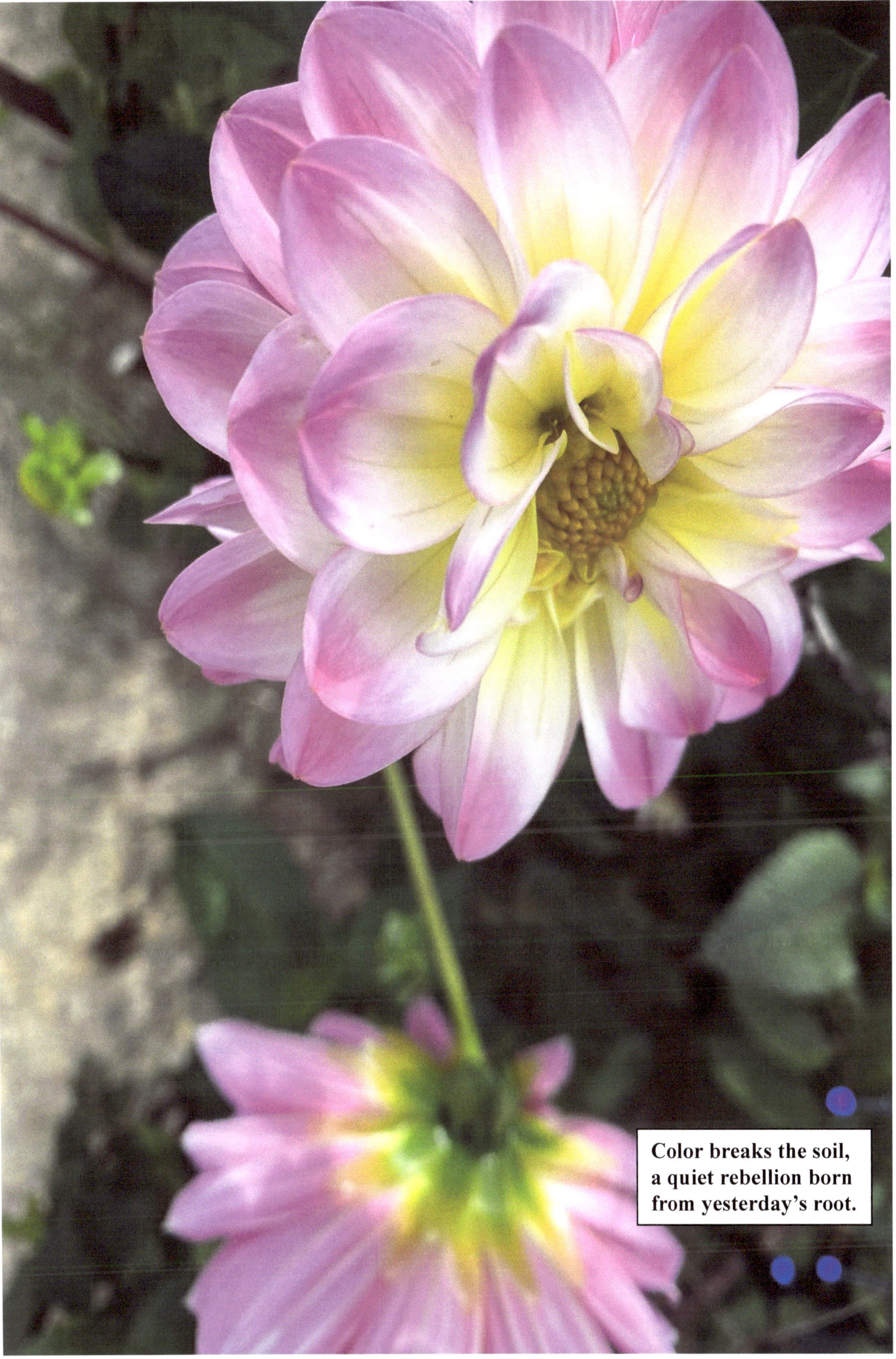
Color breaks the soil,
a quiet rebellion born
from yesterday's root.

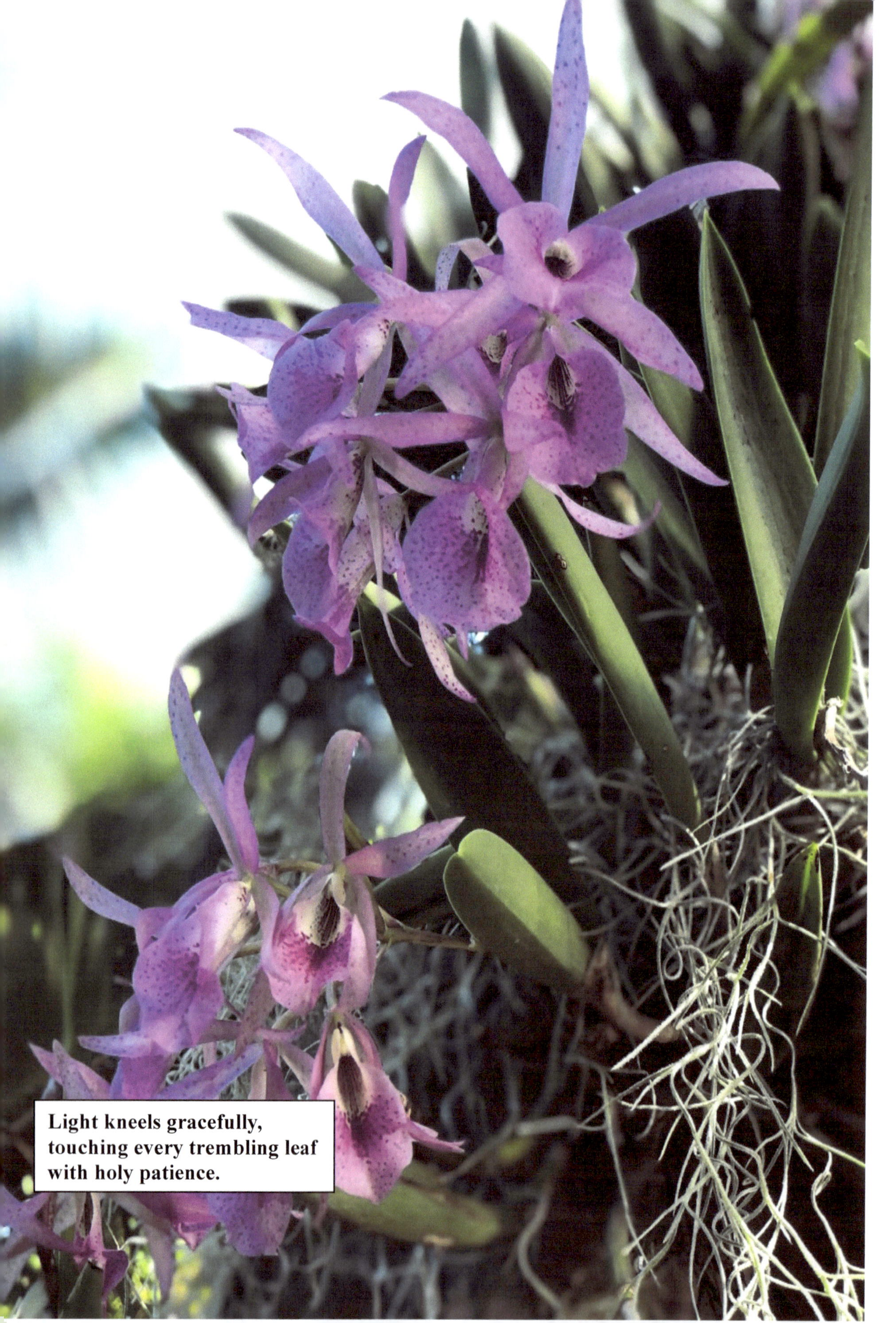

Light kneels gracefully,
touching every trembling leaf
with holy patience.

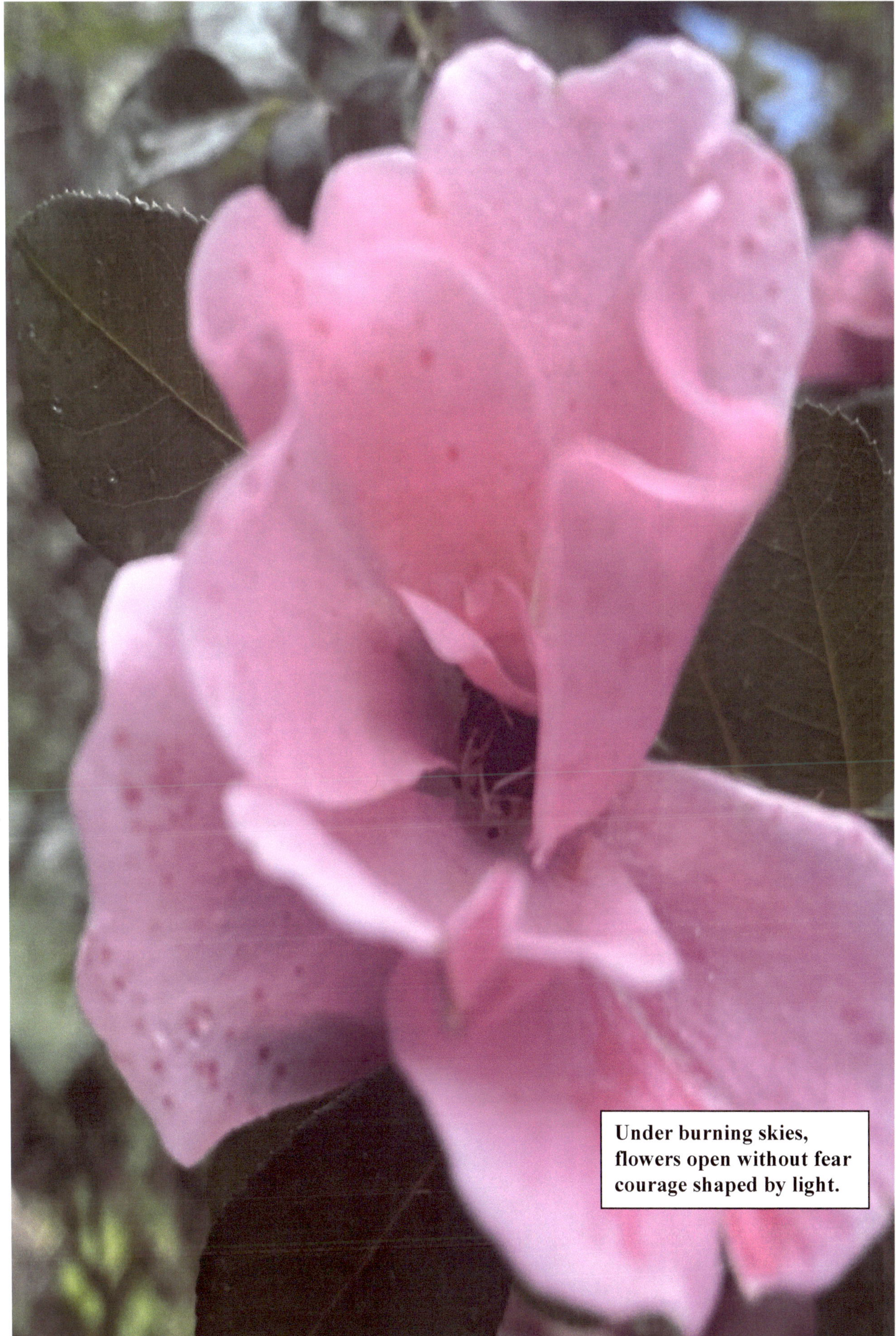
Under burning skies,
flowers open without fear
courage shaped by light.

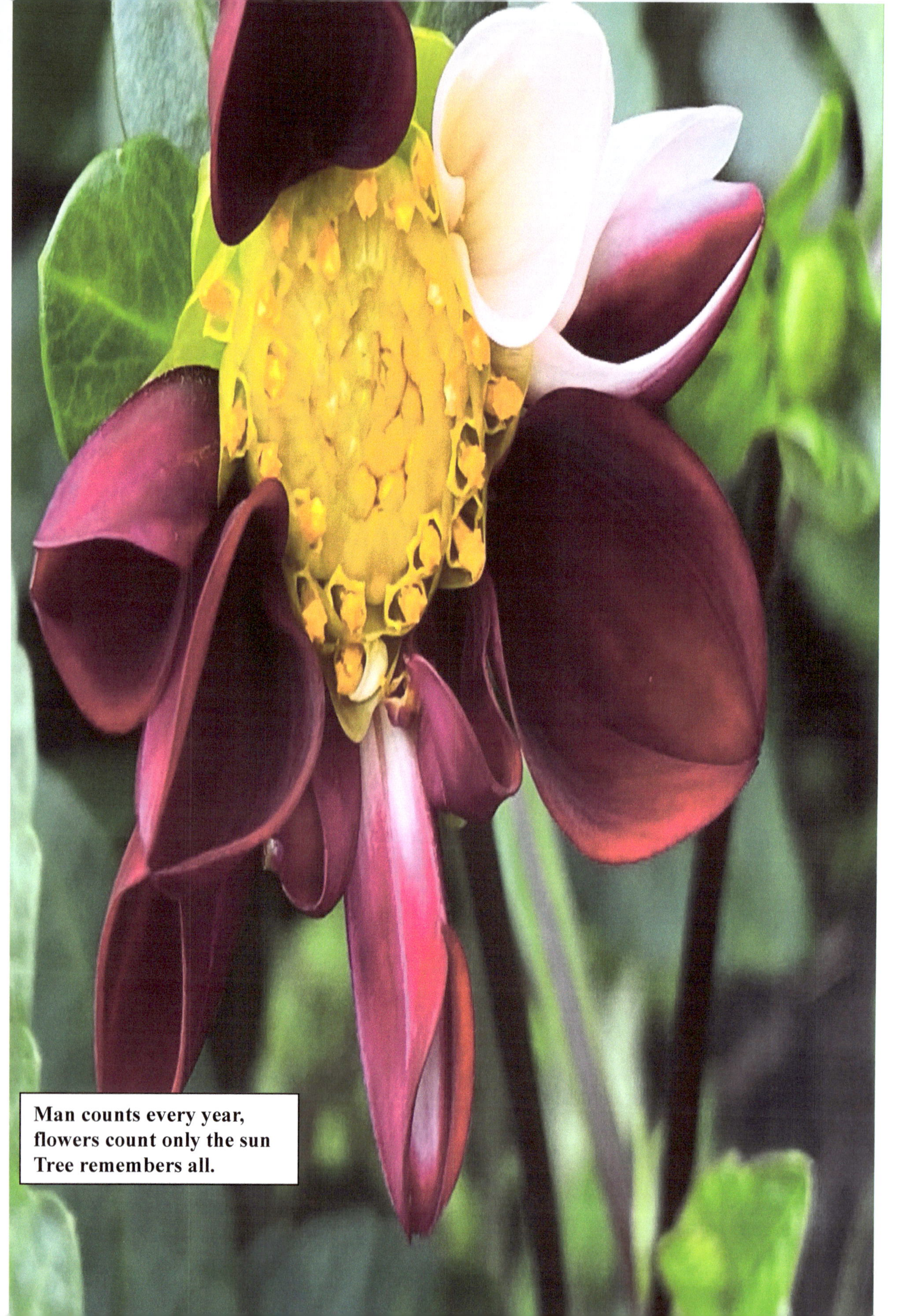
Man counts every year,
flowers count only the sun
Tree remembers all.

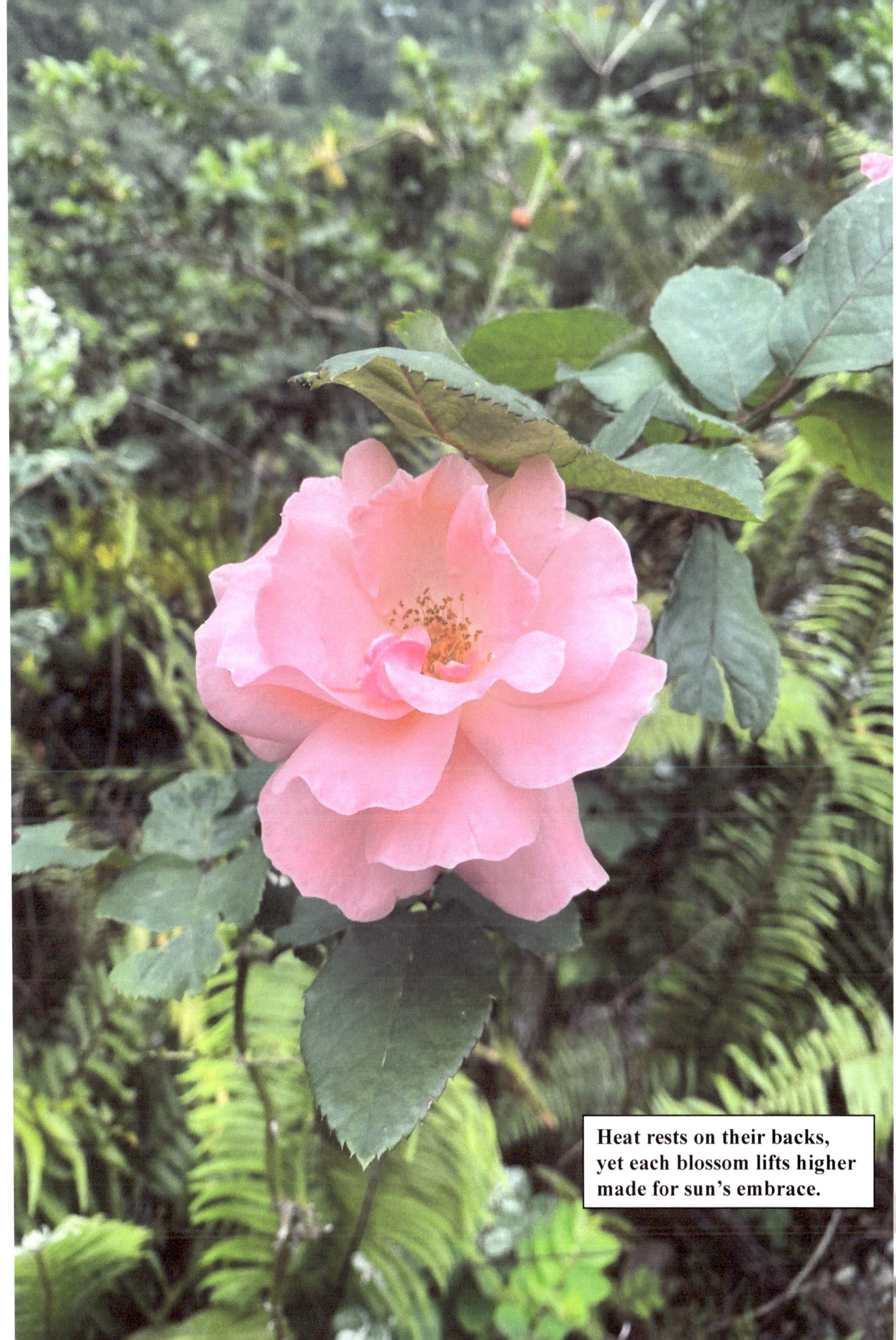
Heat rests on their backs,
yet each blossom lifts higher
made for sun's embrace.

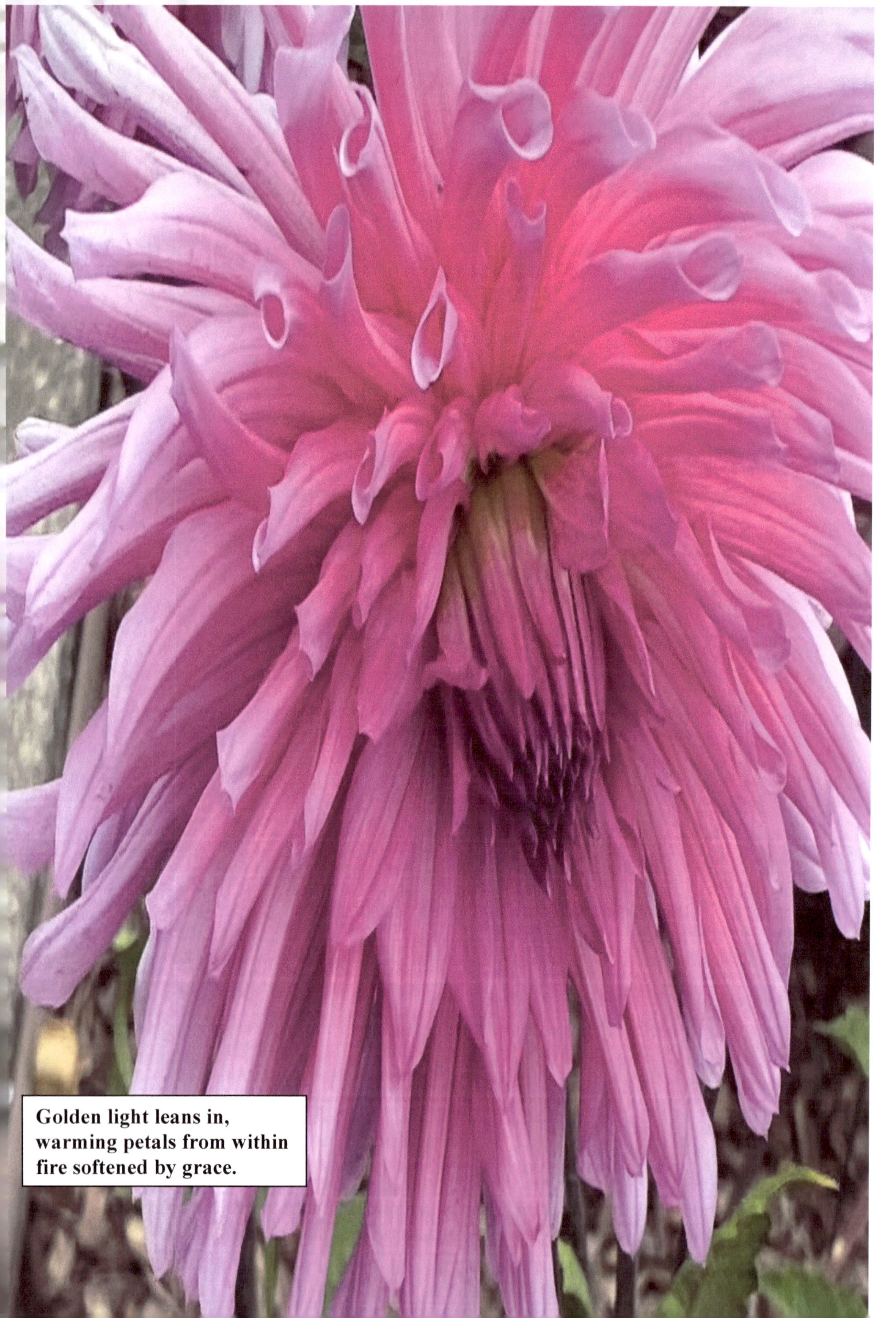

Golden light leans in,
warming petals from within
fire softened by grace.

PART III — WHAT REMAINS

If there is one truth I have learned
from standing in the same soil
for longer than anyone remembers,
it is this:

Nothing is permanent,
but nothing is truly lost.

Every bloom that falls
returns as another.
Every color that fades
becomes the memory
that teaches the next generation
how to shine.

The flowers do not understand this.
How could they?
Their lives are brief poems—
brilliant, tender,
ending just when they finally learn
the shape of their own beauty.

But I understand.
I have watched cycles
inside of cycles,
ages folding into one another
like petals pressed into a book.

I have seen whole families of flowers
go extinct,
leaving behind only
a whisper of their scent
in the soil beneath my roots.

And I have seen new blossoms appear
with faces unfamiliar to me,
carried here by the wind,

or planted by human hands
searching for something lovely
to anchor their homes to.

I stand watch through all of it.
That is my role—
not to command,
not to control,
but to bear witness.

The flowers believe
I am their God
because I am old
and unchanging
and taller than anything
they have ever known.

But age is not divinity.
Longevity is not power.
And stillness
is not holiness.

I am not a god.
I am only what the Creator designed me to be—
a keeper of stories,
a guardian of fragile lives,
a shelter for whatever dares to bloom
beneath my shadow.

I have watched humans
love and harm
with the same hands.
I have watched flowers
love and forgive
with the same petals.

Humans believe they are the gardeners,
but sometimes
it is the flowers

who teach them
how to tend a life.

Humans believe they are the caretakers,
but sometimes, it is I—
their silent witness—
who absorbs the ache of the earth
so the small ones can rest.

And the flowers—
they simply believe.
They believe in me, in the sun, in the rain,
in the good intentions
of every creature who walks near them.

Even when they are clipped too soon,
they lift their remaining days
with grace
that humbles even me.

Even when they return to the soil,
they do not grieve.
They trust the cycle—
a wisdom older than my trunk,
a faith deeper than my roots.

In my rings,
I carry the weight
of every life that ever bloomed here.
The triumphant ones.
The short-lived ones.
The ones torn out too early.
The ones planted with love.

I carry them all
because someone must remember.

This is what remains
after centuries:

the understanding
that everything the Creator made
is part of the same great breath.

Humans, flowers, rains, storms,
soil, seasons,
and even me—
the old guardian still doing my best—
we are all connected
by the simple act
of watching over one another.

So, when you close this book,
know this:

The flowers call me God
because they bloom
in the small space
where my shade meets the light.

But the miracle has never been me.
It has always been them—
the brave, short-lived wonders
who rise again, and again, and again,
teaching the world
how to begin.

And until my last leaf falls,
I will stand here,
carrying their stories,
protecting their dreams,
and honoring the Creator
who trusted me
to watch them grow.

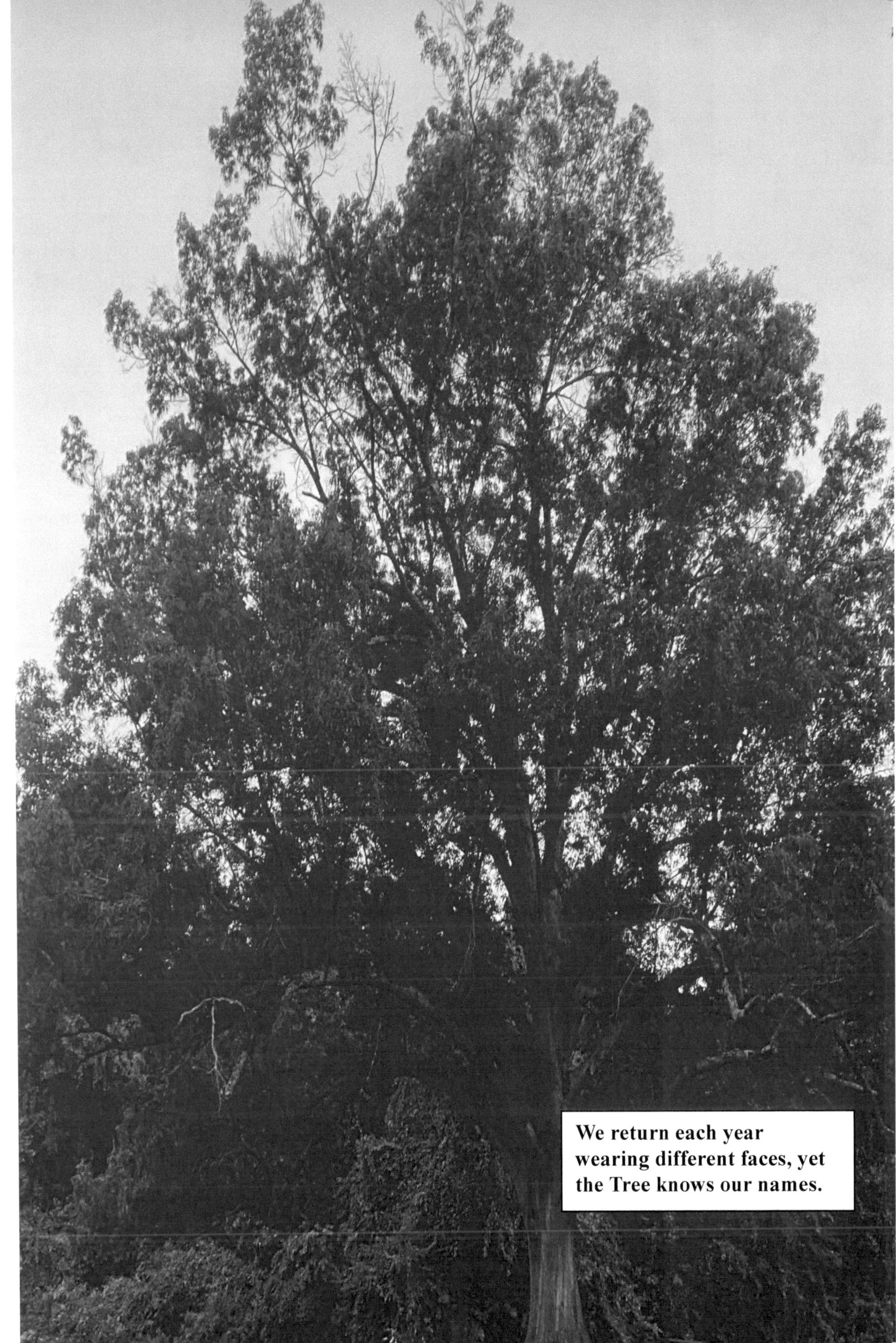
We return each year
wearing different faces, yet
the Tree knows our names.

Poet Place Book Review

What the Tree Saw is an exquisite, meditative journey told through the voice of an ancient tree who has witnessed generations of flowers, humans, storms, and seasons pass beneath its watch. With poetic clarity and spiritual weight, Olga Foreign invites readers into a garden where every petal carries memory and every bloom holds meaning.

The haiku are especially striking. They serve as emotional echoes of the images they accompany — from “Wind carries secrets, petals lean in to listen…” “Man sees only earth, flowers only branches high — Tree sees God in both”.

Visually, the book is lush. The photographs of flowers bloom with vivid color and intimate detail, each paired with a caption that deepens the reader’s sense of stillness and place.

The Tree’s voice is the true heart of the book — wise, ancient, humble, and deeply observant. Part I introduces this voice with lines like “I have stood in this soil long enough to remember what the earth felt like before your footsteps shaped it…” and continues building emotional resonance as the Tree recounts centuries of change, drought, rebirth, and human touch.

Part II, is a masterpiece of ecological memory. The Tree reflects on mutation, climate shifts, drought, human tenderness, and human carelessness — all with the humility of a being who knows he is not a god, only a witness.

Part III, is where the book becomes timeless. The Tree’s reflections on mortality, ancestry, faith, and renewal land with poetic force. The closing pages remind us that it is the flowers — fragile, fleeting, brave — who teach the world “how to begin” .

This is not just a picture book. It is not just a poem. It is not just a spiritual reflection.

It is **all three woven into one**, forming a rare work that feels both ancient and modern, personal and universal. *What the Tree Saw* stands alongside works like *The Giving Tree*, Mary Oliver’s nature poetry, and Rumi-inspired visual books — yet it carries a voice entirely its own.
It is a book to gift, to revisit, to leave on a table, to sit with quietly when the world becomes too loud.

www.ingramcontent.com/pod-product-compliance
Lightning Source LLC
LaVergne TN
LVHW072038150826
845671LV00015B/333
* 9 7 9 8 9 9 2 8 4 8 2 2 9 *